THIS IS
YOUR
DESTINY

THIS IS YOUR DESTINY

USING ASTROLOGY TO MANIFEST YOUR BEST LIFE

Aliza Kelly

ST. MARTIN'S
ESSENTIALS
NEW YORK

First published in the United States by St. Martin's Essentials, an imprint of St. Martin's Publishing Group

THIS IS YOUR DESTINY. Copyright © 2021 by Aliza Kelly. All rights reserved. Printed in the United States of America. For information, address St. Martin's Publishing Group, 120 Broadway, New York, NY 10271.

www.stmartins.com

The Library of Congress Cataloging-in-Publication Data is available upon request.

ISBN 978-1-250-76314-3 (hardcover)
ISBN 978-1-250-76315-0 (ebook)

Our books may be purchased in bulk for promotional, educational, or business use. Please contact your local bookseller or the Macmillan Corporate and Premium Sales Department at 1-800-221-7945, extension 5442, or by email at MacmillanSpecialMarkets@macmillan.com.

First Edition: 2021

10 9 8 7 6 5 4 3 2 1

GRATITUDE

Dedicated to my clients and community, teachers and guides.

Echoing from the highest mountain,
rippling through the deepest waves,
and gripping the horizon like the stubborn summer Sun:
Thank you.
Thank you.
Thank you.

CONTENTS

Astrology is more
than a practice—
it's a portal.

@alizakelly

INVITATION

YOU ARE HERE

This Is Your Destiny is an invitation for everyone, everywhere, to take an active role in consciousness. To make empowered choices that reflect your deepest truths. To show up, be present, and relish the sublime fortuity of simply being alive.

You're here, right now, and that's exactly where you need to be.

Welcome.

xx Aliza

PREFACE

THE SIREN'S SONG:
Astrology During a Pandemic

*A*t the very beginning of the COVID-19 outbreak, there was a collective scrambling. As the virus spread, cities across the United States began entering unprecedented "lockdowns" and "quarantines"—concepts that, before 2020, seemed almost exclusively literary. Against the backdrop of a rapidly escalating pandemic haphazardly managed by broken leadership, guidance was reduced to a simple, two-word directive: STAY HOME.

Usually, New York City's value isn't measured in square footage—it's measured in experience. But for the first few months of 2020, COVID-19 swarmed the city like locust: everything was covered with disease. The city, itself, was contaminated. So as essential workers slapped on makeshift protective equipment constructed from old fleece jackets and vacuum filters to assemble hospital beds in Central Park, we the people retreated to our apartments. For me, that meant—almost overnight—New York City shrunk to seven hundred square feet. And it was from that space, in my apartment, where I heard the heartbreaking wails.

Of course, New Yorkers are no strangers to noise. All day long, we move to the rhythm of an urban orchestra: teenagers yelling, cars honking, subwoofers pounding, construction sites clambering, and—in the warmer months—ice cream trucks blasting a seemingly demonic rendition of "Pop Goes the Weasel." It's cinematic, a sort of living soundtrack complete with bass and percussion and melody.

But a sick city doesn't groove—it cries. So as the virus spread and movement paused, noises began disappearing. Gone were the screaming teenagers, the honking cars, the pounding subwoofers, the cacophonous construction sites. As a New Yorker, born and raised, I've heard the city play *many* different tracks—but the one echoing across the streets in March 2020 was different. By the end of the month, the only sound remaining was the siren's solitary song.

In my apartment, my phone was vibrating hourly to remind me that COVID-19 cases were rising at exponential rates: New Yorkers were infected. They were dying. And, as if to verify the dystopian notifications, ambulances multiplied. Flooding in and out of hospitals, white boxy trucks rushed down the empty streets, sending long, piercing howls into the absence of motion, permeating the void with their looping lament. The sirens' endless wails became a sort of modern-day *moirologia*[1]: the collective cry of a city in pain.

And, in a seemingly separate universe, there was the Internet. Relegated indoors, we became dependent on social media as our lifeline. In the early days of the COVID-19 outbreak, when the virtual hive mind scrambled to adjust to this "new normal," social media was flooded with banana bread recipes and exercise routines and inspirational quotes about productivity. One, in particular, was especially taunting: "When Shakespeare was quarantined, he wrote *King Lear.* What are *you* doing with your time?"

Of course, this type of messaging didn't last long. The collective consciousness quickly agreed that "plague shaming" was *not* the right vibe. We were, after all, experiencing a shared trauma—who could *possibly* be expected to produce meaning-ful art in a global crisis? Social media quickly adopted a softer tone: Rest. Relax. Restore.

But that wasn't my reality. As I attempted to tune out the sonic suffering and mitigate an unforeseen family crisis (my grandmother—one of my closest relatives—was suddenly trapped in her nursing home, which was experiencing hundreds of COVID-19 cases), I had an astrology book to write. I was, of course, extraordinarily grateful. As the virus surged, unem-ployment followed: layoffs and furloughs and job uncertainty were painful layers of this unfathomable tragedy. And this, too, added to my own existential dread. *Why me?*

You see, *This Is Your Destiny* was born into a totally differ-ent world—in fact, my original outline for this book predates COVID-19. Once upon a time, I bounced around the city with a book proposal, shaking hands (sans hand sanitizer) with editors, and spewing ominous facts about "2020 Astrology" from an un-masked mouth.

(What made the astrology of 2020 so unique is that there were not just one but several exceptionally rare cosmic occurrences back-to-back across the Cancer-Capricorn axis—zodiac signs associated with secu-rity, tradition, and government. In fact, many of 2020's planetary hap-penings hadn't been experienced since the fall of 1517, just a few weeks after Martin Luther hammered his theses to the church door—an act that kicked off the Protestant Reformation.)

That was only ten months ago, but in the midst of a pandemic, it might as well be eight centuries ago. At the time of this writing, outerwear *without* a mask feels old-fashioned, like powdered wigs and decorative corsets—costumes from a period piece. Likewise, I feared that *This Is Your Destiny* was also an anachronism: Was this book *already* outdated, a relic from another time? Was it no longer relevant? Had my book become . . . obsolete?

I was panicking. My book deadline was approaching, I had nothing to write, and what the fuck, I couldn't stop thinking about Shakespeare and *King Lear*—I was haunted by that stupid Internet meme. As I stared at a blank document, my mind began to wander. I wanted to know more about Shakespeare's quarantine experience: What was the square footage of his London flat? Did he feel claustrophobic? Were there sirens? Did he think about the Greek wailers, too? But mostly, I wanted to know if he, also, questioned the relevancy of his work: Was the iconic William Shakespeare wallowing in existential dread? Was he worried about *King Lear*'s potential insignificance?

So this is what I found out: though it's true that Shakespeare penned *King Lear* during the bubonic plague, Professor Mary Bly of Fordham University noted that it's highly unlikely he wrote the famed tragedy in London proper. According to Professor Bly, during a plague outbreak (which were quite common in those days), anyone with class or privilege would flee to the country. Likewise, Shakespeare—who was *not* a starving artist—almost certainly wrote *King Lear* whilst gazing out upon a gorgeous, bucolic vista, complete with acreage and sunshine and virtually no proto-ambulances whatsoever.[2] *(Damnit, Willy—I thought we were in this together!)*

It's unclear, however, exactly when he wrote *King Lear.* At that time, plague outbreaks would occur every few years, and because Shakespeare didn't formally date this particular work, scholars look to clues within the text—such as dialogue surrounding the solar and lunar eclipses—to gauge timing.

Wait, what? Come again?

Eclipses?

Yes, that's correct. Sure, any history buff (or ambitious high school student) knows that Shakespeare's work is *filled* with celestial references: Romeo and Juliet are "star-cross'd lovers," a character is told to "obey the moon" in *Winter's Tale,* and even Mars' oblong retrograde is discussed in *Henry IV Part I.* In fact, throughout all of Shakespeare's thirty-seven plays, there are quite literally *hundreds* of astrological references.[3] And, in *King Lear* (Act 1, Scene 2), a conversation between two primary characters directly references topical astrological happenings: "These late eclipses in the sun and moon portend no good to us." (I.2.100–101).

Maybe it was the lack of sleep, but when I stumbled upon this particular dialogue, it felt profoundly meaningful. I abide by the philosophy that there are no coincidences (a concept I'll unpack in great detail later in this book), so I knew I had to uncover more.

These days, it's easy to find out what's going on in the cosmos. Within seconds, a quick Internet search can confirm the current lunar phase, whether Mercury is retrograde, or when the next eclipse is scheduled to serve up its signature chaos. Although we may not realize it, being actively aware of *all* planetary movement at any given moment is a very contemporary way of interacting with the stars. For the majority of human history, astrology wasn't based on what we were reading on our smartphones, but rather, what we were actually *seeing* in the sky.

Although eclipses aren't rare (they occur three to seven times each year), actually *witnessing* one—especially a total solar eclipse (when the Sun is completely blocked by the Moon)—is quite remarkable. Total solar eclipses are only visible for a short amount of time from very specific locations known as the "path of totality." It's a big deal to be on the path of totality. In fact, thousands of years of folklore link the path of totality with socio-political transformation (for instance, back on August 2, 1133, it was believed that the total solar eclipse over

England coincided with the death of Henry I and subsequent political unrest). So, on March 7, 1598, as Londoners watched in awe as the Sun disappeared beneath the Moon's silhouette, everyone—including William Shakespeare—wanted to know what was going to happen. After all, change *was* inevitable.

So *King Lear* wasn't just penned during a plague, it was also written in the shadow of an eclipse. I mean, #same. Back in my seven-hundred-square-foot apartment, the parallels were striking. On August 21, 2017, the "Great American Eclipse" forged a path of totality that spanned the entire continental United States, crossing diagonally from South Carolina to Oregon. And it was a big fucking deal. In fact, I wrote about this major celestial event in my first weekly column in *Allure* magazine:

> "The solar eclipse will completely obstruct the sun for two minutes and forty seconds, resulting in an incredible astronomical visual display. Astrologically, however, the impact of this solar eclipse will extend much longer than a few minutes of blackout—it has the potential to change our world forever."[4]

Back to the present, and my computer's desktop has officially devolved into a virtual bulletin board mapping a crime scene. Instead of writing my book—this book—I'm obsessively trying to track cosmic correspondence, collecting clues to determine whether the 2017 Great American Eclipse really did foreshadow the 2020 pandemic. And, if so, did the 1598 "Total Eclipse of the Sun"[5] in England also herald the 1603 death of Queen Elizabeth I, the end of the Tudor dynasty, and that particularly fatal plague outbreak that prompted Shakespeare to flee London and write *King Lear*?

Maybe.

But I also discovered something else. Through this unexpected time travel, I reconnected with the very sensibility that first guided me to astrology so many moons ago: insatiable curiosity. Weaving centuries like constellations, astrology transcends apartments and sirens and pandemics. My connection to the cosmos is built on imagination and creativity and wonder. The stars are mirrors speckled across an incomprehensible landscape—what other domain could possibly reflect the bizarre profundity of consciousness? Or the depth of resilience? Or the interconnectivity of us all?

This Is Your Destiny isn't a book about what astrology is—it's about what astrology *does.* It's about how you can use the cosmos as a resource to transform your reality. It's an homage to the fact that astrology is more than a practice; it's a portal. And, this book is your passport to another dimension.

So, dear reader, what does the world look like today? What year is it? Has everything changed? Are you listening to sweet melodies? Or heartbreaking sirens? Or are you wrapped in velvety silence, cozy on your couch with a crocheted blanket and aromatic herbal tea? All is calm.

No matter where this book finds you—whether you're writing the next *King Lear* or just trying to get through the day—know that the cosmos are yours to define. Let the Sun and Moon and stars and solar systems and galaxies and space beyond your wildest dreams illuminate the path forward. Let this moment be every moment—infinite.

—May 2020, New York City

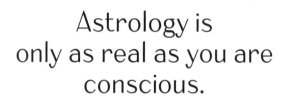

✦

Astrology is
only as real as you are
conscious.

@alizakelly

ON ANONYMITY

Please note that names have been changed to maintain the privacy of my clients, friends, and relatives. Specific personal details (such as age, occupation, or geographic location) have been omitted, adjusted, and reimagined to both maintain anonymity and narrative flow. Stories are the amalgamation of many client sessions. In other words, they're all of us.

Astrology isn't
prescriptive,
it's perspective.

@alizakelly

INTRODUCTION

COSMOS AND CHAOS

For someone who's obsessed with tracking time, you'd think I'd be better at keeping it.

On one hand, I'm a fastidious record-keeper with a photographic memory who snaps facts like Polaroids. I demand accountability, so I always save my receipts. But I'm *also* a mutable, ethereal poet whose internal clock resembles a Dalí painting. Running behind schedule? No problem! Nothing is real, everything is a construct, and life is but a spiral. Chat later!

Sometimes these qualities feel like mortal enemies. They are, after all, deeply contradictory. But whenever my harsh punctual nature tries to control my free spirit, or my dreamy artistic soul instructs my inner-disciplinary to "loosen up," I'm left frustrated, annoyed, and even *more* stratified. It hasn't been easy, but in time, I've learned that these qualities—rigidity and fluidity—don't negate each other. Within my person, they are both equally true, equally important, and equally beautiful. They exist simultaneously.

You can see these dueling dynamics play out in real time by scrolling through my digital photo library, which contains hundreds (thousands?) of nearly identical images of my phone's locked screen as I attempt to screenshot a specific time and date—a futile attempt to track significant moments. Futile because these screenshots have no context: I don't label or categorize them, so I have virtually no idea what event I was even trying to timestamp. Was it a powerful feeling? A spiritual breakthrough? Numerological synchronicity? My logical mind begs for an explanation, but my inner-mystic says it doesn't matter. The sheer act of *capturing time* offers an incredible adrenaline rush. Screenshots are cheap shots of dopamine: I love the way the phone lights up bright white, simulating the blinding flash of an analog camera, complete with the fabricated sound of a shutter's manual *click*.

Do you remember those? Film cameras?

These days, everything's some type of simulation: an imprint of an imprint of an imprint. This is, of course, exactly why astrology performs so well on social media: astrology *is* an ancient meme—it *isn't* the entire universe but it *represents* it. The microcosm and the macrocosm folded together.

The word "cosmos" is derived from the ancient Greek "kosmos," meaning both "order" and "universe." Its dual-definition is pretty literal: philosophers believed that all organic systems (humanity, animals, nature, as well as the planets, stars, and galaxies) flowed in perfect harmony. They envisioned life animated through patterns, mirrors, and feedback loops. Everything is symmetrical. Everything is cyclical. Each moment is every moment—within a single screenshot, an entire existence.

Astrologers track life through birth charts (Table 1). The birth chart (also called a "natal chart") is a two- dimensional representation of the sky at someone's (or something's) exact moment of arrival—it's calculated through time, date, and location. Filled with shapes and symbols and geometry, birth charts are intricate diagrams. In fact, the first time you examine your birth chart, it may feel like you're looking at hieroglyphics—the iconography requires fluency in a completely different language. But, through practice, you'll discover what makes a birth chart so extraordinary: it's a gateway to the universe. Your universe.

Of all the extensions of my astrological practice, nothing feels quite as sacred as exploring clients' birth charts. Tucked within the folds of esoteric symbolism is an individual's entire life story, which is really a collection of many epic narratives, too many to count. One common misconception about astrology is that it's dogmatic—that the stars and planets *tell* you who you are through stereotypical characteristics and banal attributes. But the cosmos aren't literal, they're metaphors. Sure, the planets are *really* occupying certain positions, but their meaning is interpretative.

Astrology, like a camera, is an instrument designed to shift your perspective. Using the cosmos' wide-angle lens, astrology enables you to create powerful depictions—snapshots—of different dimensions of your life. It, quite literally, gives you the space to unpack your complexities and explore multidimensionality through cyclical (as opposed to linear) time. In my work as an astrologer, it's the tool I use to help clients visualize their realities through an expanded vantage.

✹

I find astrology to be a full-body experience. To access the full range of the cosmos during my one-on-one client sessions, I need to engage every cell of my being, simultaneously listening, processing, questioning, reflecting, and interpreting. Plus, my bullshit meter needs to be fully charged and perfectly calibrated to ensure that we're speaking the truth, the whole truth, and nothing but the truth.

To clarify, I'm *not* bringing my bullshit meter to sessions because my clients are a bunch of liars. It's actually the exact opposite: astrology is a practice in veracity, so my clients—like me—are also adamantly seeking truth. Through astrology, we practice critical thinking: we don't just accept realities "as is," we trace them to their root.

How did the cycle start?
Why does it exist?
What does it mean?

I'm so profoundly grateful that, over the years, I've had the privilege of working with thousands of clients, Although each journey is unique, each private session has made my practice deeper, richer, and more complex. The power behind this energetic interconnectivity crystallized as I realized that within each client's story is *everyone's* story. Like matryoshka dolls, we live nested in others' narratives. People—like zodiac signs and planets—are also symbols and, as I synthesized thousands of conversations, even greater wisdoms began to unfold.

Accordingly, my practice began shifting. What would happen if we pushed the boundaries of astrological interpretation even further, using it to not just *reflect* truth but also *direct* energy? And what if we *converted* these truths into intentional energy, empowering us to expand our horizon beyond what we ever imagined possible? Could astrology become a vehicle for self-actualization?

Manifestation is one of those trendy terms that is thrown around frequently, but rarely defined, which I think is primarily because it's not an easy concept to explain. When I discovered the link between astrology and self-actualization, I realized I needed to be very explicit about what manifestation is (and what it is not): **In my practice, manifestation is the process of instituting change by opening a portal between the astral and physical realms** (dimensions that will be defined in great detail shortly) (Art 1: Manifestation Flow). Manifestation requires equal parts energy (internal force), intentionality (desired outcome), and action (tangible output), which means manifestation cannot occur passively. **You—your free will, your agency, your tenacity—catalyze manifestation.** It's also important to note that manifestation isn't just a snap of the fingers: It's magick, not magic (magick is the art of channeling and directing energy, whereas magic is performative illusions). Likewise, manifestation takes time to unfold, requiring both patience and—believe it or not—structure.

A rebel at heart, I spent many, *many* years breaking rules of all shapes and sizes. From dress codes to curfews to bedtimes to due dates, I believed that any type of boundary was inherently soul crushing. At first, my relationship with astrology seemed to be another act of defiance—it was, after all, non-conformist in nature—but, ironically, I came to discover that astrology is built on exactitudes, parameters, and protocols. From planetary speeds (how quickly a celestial body completes its orbit) to essential dignities (the association of planets and signs), astrology is technical, and—for a practice so often dismissed as dubious—shockingly precise.

Yet somehow, despite my innate disdain for rules, I found myself accepting—yes, even *enjoying*—the boundaries embedded in the cosmos; structures are containers for creative interpretation. What's more, the organic flow of the celestial bodies provides dynamic context for our natural human cycles. For instance, the Moon (symbolizing internal experiences) rotates every twenty-eight days, helping us visualize the wax and wane of our emotions over the course of a month. The Sun, connected to external character, moves through a 365-day cycle, enabling us to track the development of our identity on an annual basis. Mercury (representing communication) rotates every 88 days, Venus (associated with values) 225 days, Mars (embodying action) 687 days. As we travel deeper into our solar system, the planets shift from "personal" (that is, directly impacting individual life experiences) to "generational," correlating with larger social transformation tracked in epochs that transcend a human lifetime. On the other side of the asteroid belt, planets make even larger orbits: twelve years for Jupiter, twenty-nine years for Saturn, eighty-four years for Uranus, 165 years for Neptune, 248 years for Pluto (Table 2).

All planetary rotations have distinctive milestones. Aspects—that is, the relationships between planets in the sky—serve as checkpoints: every journey begins with a *conjunction*, reaches the quarter at a *square*, and halfway at an *opposition*. Aspects anchor us in time, place, and space, offering invaluable context as we move through our own personal stories.

Some cycles are embodied biologically (the Moon's orbit corresponds with menses), culturally (in *astrospeak*, birthdays are referred to as "Solar Returns," marking the completion of the Sun's cycle), or allegorically (we experience the "Saturn Return" in our late twenties, which is a notoriously challenging and transformative time). It's important to remember that the planets are *always* in motion, which means we're *always* moving through cycles. Likewise, even if we can't define the orbit by name, astrology reminds us that life is never static—flow is constant on a celestial and cellular level.

By cultivating a rich relationship with the astrological cycles, I discovered that manifestation—that is, deliberately catalyzing change through intention—is amplified when linked to cosmic patterns. Through astrology, we expand our perspective, enabling us to visualize possibilities, potential, and promise outside our present-day vantage. And, in understanding that we are constantly moving through cycles, and our *realities* are constantly in bloom (seeding, sprouting, flowering, fruiting, dispersing, germinating), it's clear that transformation isn't just possible, it's *inevitable*. **Accordingly, by aligning our manifestations with this organic unfolding, we can thoughtfully *direct* our growth toward our dreams, synthetizing journey and desire.**

This Is Your Destiny is a collection of stories, weaved together to form a single constellation. Within these pages, you'll find different tools: my personal experiences as both an astrologer and human being, clients' extraordinary tales, mystical and esoteric wisdom, as well as custom manifestation techniques to help you connect with your truth. So whether you're a seasoned mystic who's looking to expand their practice or a fledgling stargazer just preparing to take flight, this book is intended to meet you exactly where you are. It will reflect exactly what you need, so you just stay right there. *This Is Your Destiny* will come to you.

✳

This Is Your Destiny is divided into nine chapters, seven of which address a major area of life: identity, money, community, intimacy, career, challenges, and spirituality. Together, we'll explore each theme from a multidimensional perspective. We'll discuss not just what that concept represents, but also *why* it plays such a vital role in self-actualization. I'll share stories and offer powerful manifestation exercises. By the time you complete each chapter, you'll not only have a deeper understanding of how that topic informs your consciousness, but also how to identify your true desires *relative* to that area of life, and, accordingly, bring them to fruition.

But this isn't a quick fix. This book isn't a Band-Aid or a glue gun or a stapler. It's a comprehensive deep dive into virtually every aspect of your consciousness. *This Is Your Destiny* isn't going to solve your problems—only you can do that—but it will help you cultivate an ongoing practice, enabling you to visualize your life through this expanded vantage. Everything is connected: improving your romantic relationships is about renegotiating your self-worth, achieving professional success is about cultivating an abundance-based mentality, coping with life's most difficult circumstances is about building a rich, spiritual inner world. And it's all available here, organized into chapters, splayed out as words on a page, and embedded within a single book. Magick.

WRITTEN IN THE STARS

I was born on August 18, 1989, at 5:28 PM in New York City. A few days later, my mother received a special package in the mail. Tucked neatly inside a large manila envelope was my birth chart—the astrological blueprint to my destiny.

My uncle Jeremy met my biological aunt in the early 1970s at Binghamton University. After some time living up and down the East Coast, the two gradually made their way to Orange County, California, where Jeremy opened a successful law practice.

But Jeremy wasn't just a lawyer, he was also a Sagittarius. And true to the archetype of this erudite fire sign, Jeremy was an extremely gifted astrologer. So, when I was just a few days old, Jeremy—armed with a protractor, ephemeris, and a box of multicolored Bic pens—carefully illustrated my own mystical roadmap by rendering a hand-calculated birth chart. (These days, because astrology software is affordable and accessible, most astrologers use software to render birth charts—so the fact that Jeremy prepared my chart manually, the "old-fashioned way" makes it extra special.) Each corner is decorated with psychedelic, celestial motifs, reflecting the four elements of astrology: fire, earth, water, and air. As I look at the paper now, I can see where he pressed the pen deep into the page, as if to emphasize certain noteworthy attributes.

But Jeremy was very sick. I only have one memory of Jeremy—and I'm not even sure if it counts as a "memory"—it's actually just a still image. I can visualize Jeremy in the living room of his house. He's sitting upright in a hospital bed, which was propped on a parquet platform flanked by three large bay windows (serious 1980s architecture moment). California light is flooding through the floor-to-ceilings windows—I imagine it's midmorning, maybe about 10 A.M.?— spilling across the stark white hospital sheets. Jeremy's hair is black. Enveloped by the Sun's rays, this mental snapshot evokes ease and tranquility, a sensory contradiction to the foreboding medical equipment.

Jeremy died on August 24, 1993, just a few days after my fourth birthday. Believe it or not, I actually have a memory of this, too—though this one plays like a movie. Set in my childhood apartment, the memory starts with me walking toward my mother, who was facing away from me, staring out the window. It's dawn. The sky is electric pink. Then, I'm standing next to her. Although I don't recall her telling me that Jeremy died, that information must have somehow been communicated, because I specifically remember pointing to a bright star hovering low in the sky and attempting to comfort her by saying, "That's him."

Does this memory feel *suspiciously* cinematic? That the four-year-old me—who would grow up to become a professional astrologer—attempted to soothe my grieving mother by linking soul and star? I thought so, too, which is why—prior to including that particular anecdote in this book—I tested the validity of the memory by calculating the sunrise charts for both August 24 and August 25, 1993. Believe it or not, the poignant recollection totally checks out: on those days, Venus was in a "morning star" phase, which means the planet was rising *before* the Sun and, at dawn, would have been visible (and extremely prominent) from the window of my apartment building.

But alas, at four years old, I couldn't foresee how drastically my life was about to change. From what I've pieced together over the years, it seems that my mother's grief created a sharp wedge in her relationship with my father and, by August 1996, my parents were suiting up for what would quickly devolve into an exhausting, bitter, and deeply traumatic divorce and subsequent custody battle that sent them both into emotional and economic destitution, and me, my parents' only child, into my first black hole.

THE BLACK HOLES

So far, my life has fallen apart four times: at seven, when my parents divorced; at ten, when my mother was first diagnosed with cancer; between the ages of thirteen and fifteen, when I tried to escape; and between the ages of twenty-three and twenty-seven, when I learned to surrender.

On my last day of first grade, on the woolen gray rug at the corner of the room, my teacher invited students to share their summer plans. "My parents are getting divorced," I proudly announced to the class. I noted my teacher's face—twisted, uncomfortable—as I volunteered this information, indicating that perhaps this *wasn't* the exciting adventure my parents' promised.

My mom's new apartment was a lot smaller than the one I grew up in, but it was right across the street from—what I didn't realize—would be my brand-new school. And it was in the first few weeks of second grade that I really began to feel the chaos. Divorce didn't just mean my parents didn't want to live together anymore, it meant they hated each other. It meant war. My parents would pick me up from school, late, wearing their courtroom best. My mom had started smoking and my dad had met a new, significantly younger woman who would, within that school year, become pregnant with my half-sister, marry my father, and become my stepmother. I knew no one at my new school and—overwhelmed by this unfamiliar social environment—struggled to make friends, quickly becoming the target for bullies. One girl named Helene would squeeze my cheeks until they bled. I wonder what she's doing now.

The divorce and custody battle finally came to a close in 1998, when both of my parents ran out of money. The judge ordered "joint custody," which meant that Monday and Tuesday I was at my mother's apartment, Wednesday and Thursday I was at my father's, and each weekend (including Fridays) alternated. I was constantly in motion—but I was floundering. I couldn't finish my homework because the book I needed to read was at my dad's, but I was at my mom's. I wanted to wear red for my school's Valentine's Day party, but my favorite magenta sweater was at my mom's, and now I was at my dad's. Nothing was where it needed to be. Everything was everywhere. Mayhem reigned supreme.

Things were hectic, but by the time I was in fifth grade, I had begun to find my footing. I had started experimenting with style and music, and having an unconventional family seemed to fit my increasingly nonconformist attitude. And then, one day, I went to my grandparents' house after school because my mom had a doctor's appointment. Everything was normal, until I realized that I had been playing the Sims a lot longer than usual. *What time was it? Where was my mom?* Something was wrong. I could hear my grandparents' whispering—by this point, I knew adult whispering meant trouble. I pressed a cup against the wall to listen—a technique I'd learned from one of my favorite detectives, *Harriet the Spy.* Unfortunately, it seemed to work much better in the movie. I heard nothing but muffled noises.

The rest of that evening is a blur—time is stretched and distorted and my retrospective adult-mind pokes holes in the accuracy of certain details. But the big reveal was as sharp and painful and shattering now, over twenty years later, as it was that night. Fast-forward to some hours later, my mother, finally at my grandparents' apartment, is sitting at the kitchen table and I'm splayed out sobbing on the linoleum kitchen floor. The atmosphere is tight, hot, claustrophobic—sweat on the back of your neck. The sound is industrial, like the caustic hum of an ancient generator. The tone is amber: bright and disorienting. My mom was diagnosed with breast cancer.

"But don't start telling people—it's not their business," my mother said in a stern, unfamiliar voice, "especially your father. He doesn't need to know."

At that moment, my ten-year-old brain—which had, in the past few years, already begun to master compartmentalization—went into hyperdrive. Honoring my mother's wishes, I kept her illness secret. I didn't tell my father about the radiation. Or the chemotherapy. Or the double-mastectomy. Or the plastic bags on the side of her bra that filled with blood. And I didn't tell my father about the recurrence in 2003. Or the recurrence in 2005. Or the pain medication, or the chemotherapy, or the tremendous anxiety that seeped through my subconscious like carbon dioxide. I didn't say a word.

By the time I was in high school, my mom's apartment building, including our unit, was infested with mice. She would set traps around the kitchenette, catching one occasionally, but was too sick to truly address the situation. The unspoken agreement was that each of us—my mother and myself—would stay in our respective bedrooms with the doors closed. Out of sight, out of mind.

Interestingly, my father's house (he now lived in Gowanus, Brooklyn) was infested with rodents, too—but only in my bedroom. At night, with the lights off, they would scamper up inside walls and across the ceiling. I could hear their claws and their teeth and their squeaks.

But here, too, there was nothing that could be done. You see, my bedroom at my father's house wasn't *actually* a bedroom—it was a hallway off the kitchen that was built as an illegal extension by the previous owner. And, because it wasn't "to code," my dad casually explained that subway rats (subway rats!) would *accidentally* fall into the extension, get trapped in the drywall, and eventually die. Yes, death was the sole consolation—and he was right. Every few days, the scratching was followed by silence and, soon, my hallway-bedroom would fill with the smell of putrid decomposition, which my stepmother tried to conceal with patchouli incense.

I hate the smell of patchouli.

I, too, was slipping through the cracks. Between my mother's illness and my father's disconnect, I was decaying. By the time I started high school, I had already developed a full-fledged eating disorder, was sexually active, smoked a pack of cigarettes a day, and started experimenting with drugs. Hard ones.

What happened between the ages of fourteen and seventeen I'll share in more detail later on, but by the time I was a senior in high school, let's just say I was ready for a fresh start. College was the light at the end of the tunnel. Going away to undergrad, I thought, was an opportunity to erase the past and start anew—transcending chaos and isolation and subway rats.

I was thrilled when I was accepted into my first-choice school, Carleton College, a small liberal arts school in rural Minnesota. Everything about Carleton seemed so *pure*; there was even a historic building on campus called Dacie Moses House where students could go to bake chocolate chip cookies. I already felt so jaded and weathered, and I hoped, perhaps, Carleton would allow me to embrace the innocence absent from my adolescence.

So, when I packed up my bags to begin a new chapter in the wholesome Midwest I only brought what seemed appropriate. My idea was to leave all of my toxic tendencies in New York and, in Minnesota, reinvent myself completely. In college, I planned to become the *best* version of myself. There was no need to tell my smart, well-groomed collegiate friends about my dark, destructive past. No way! I didn't want to overcomplicate my narrative—I wanted my story to be nice and neat and linear. I wanted it to make sense. I wanted to be normal.

Piece by piece, I began omitting parts of my identity that felt too divergent or contradictory or shameful—a little erasure here, a little white lie there. Thoughtful "editing" was totally fine! But over the years, all of those half-truths compounded. It became hard to keep track of what was fact, fiction, or full-on fabrication and, by the time I moved to Los Angeles in 2013, I had totally lost touch with any semblance of truth.

The next thing I knew, I was getting sucked into another black hole—only this time, I began exploring the stars.

CONNECTING THE DOTS

Chaos created the universe and, since the dawn of civilization, people have navigated uncertainty by projecting order onto the stars and planets. When I moved to Los Angeles all my rickety infrastructure began to give way. Within a matter of weeks I lost my job, boyfriend, and—one afternoon—my Craigslist roommate decided to disappear, taking all the furniture, leaving no rent money, and never contacting me again. So, I did what any perplexed human does: I looked up my horoscope.

Keep in mind that—at this point—I did *not* know that my late uncle Jeremy was an astrologer, or that somewhere, among old papers and photographs, my hand-calculated birth chart was beginning to unfold. But now, as I tried to make sense of the scotch-taped sculpture that was my life, my interest in astrology ramped up with incredible velocity. Everything was so fucking messy; astrology was the only thing that made sense.

Early in 2014, I flew back to New York to visit my mom. At her apartment, the one with the mice, I told her all about my newfound passion for the cosmos, how I started to research my birth chart, and that I wasn't just a Leo. "That's just my Sun sign," I proudly explained, "there are, in fact, dozens of other planets and zodiac signs. Did you know that my Moon is in Pisces?"

"Oh, well, what about your Pluto?" my mother casually remarked, "Jeremy was fascinated by that placement in your chart."

Huh? I didn't know what she was talking about.

"Your uncle Jeremy—he was *so* into astrology! He did your birth chart when you were born. You know that, right?"

Um. No, this was brand-new information.

She disappeared into her bedroom and, just a few moments later, returned with an old, discolored manila envelope. Passing it to me, I peered inside and carefully removed the contents. And there it was, in pristine condition. The birth chart Jeremy had rendered—untouched since 1989.

Unsurprisingly, my birth chart is complicated and challenging and riddled with friction. Between my Capricorn Ascendant, Eighth House stellium (including Leo Sun conjunct South Node with a 0° orb) that opposes my Second House Pisces Moon, Twelfth House stellium, Chiron in Cancer conjunct my Descendant, Pluto in Scorpio conjunct my Midheaven, and dozens upon dozens of other "hard" aspects, my birth chart is a serious pressure cooker.

But, uncovering the stress of my chart actually felt like a relief. Finally, something *confirmed* what I had been experiencing my whole life. Things hadn't been easy, and now, I had the birth chart to prove it. The birth chart reflected the *real* me, the *whole* me, the *multidimensional* me. There were no fractures or fragments or delusions—illustrated among the stars and planets of an ever-expanding universe, all my truths had more than enough room to stretch out, take up space, and exist simultaneously. Through astrology, I saw myself as the cosmos: complex, mysterious, and out-of-this-world.

And, through the language of astrology, I started to find my voice. It gave me the confidence to embrace myself fully and completely—to tell bigger stories. To call out the pain. Rather than truncate myself to fit a bite-sized, cookie cutter mold, I began to explore the nearly infinite expressions of my reality. Instead of embracing only *certain* aspects of myself and discarding the rest, I began exploring the totality of my person—the full 360° of my birth chart. What does it mean to be a passionate, playful, spotlight-loving Leo Sun and *also* a stern, hardworking, skeptical Capricorn Rising? How do I communicate the complex feelings of my empathetic, abstract Pisces Moon through my logical, systematic Virgo Mercury? Challenges became opportunities to explore my innate multidimensionality with compassionate curiosity. And, when I was no longer afraid of the hard stuff, it became a lot easier to face my fears, enabling me to become more honest, and—dare I say—whole.

But, let me clarify, this process took time. And effort . . . a lot of effort. There's no denying that it's *much* easier to feign ignorance than face the facts, especially when the truth is painful. I had spent my entire life operating under the assumption that I couldn't possibly embrace the totality of my experience—it was scary to admit what I truly wanted, and it was terrifying to accept what was actually happening. But, through astrology, I discovered that reality is constantly in motion. Accepting that change is inevitable meant I could simultaneously accept my current circumstances (as uncomfortable as they may be) and *simultaneously* treat my hopes and dreams and wishes with the utmost reverence, creating a bridge between past, present, and future.

What I also discovered is that I was actually *afraid* of my truth. Despite my rebellious, nonconformist spirit, society's harsh standards had still infiltrated my psyche. At what point did I stop believing in myself? Self-doubt and insecurities compound, and—with an already precarious infrastructure—I could be critically wounded by even the smallest paper cuts.

It became increasingly clear that the first step to improving my circumstances was *believing* my circumstances could be improved, and, in order to do that, I had to work on restoring my confidence. By practicing veracity—that is, fearless truth-telling—I took accountability for my reality, identifying what was (or wasn't) working, how I *actually* felt in different situations, and what I genuinely aspired to achieve. Authenticity is empowering. Through learning about myself under the auspices of astrology, I began building self-esteem. With sustainable, self-generated validation, I discovered that I had the ability to have agency over my journey—the gateway to manifestation.

And, now, I'm ready to share these wisdoms with you. Because this is *your* destiny, and you deserve to enjoy the ride.

There are
no coincidences.

@alizakelly

ONE

ASTROLOGY AND MANIFESTATION

But What About My Zodiac Sign?

Are you a mysterious Scorpio? Excellent, I'm glad you're here!

Or maybe you're an exploratory Sagittarius, ready to go on the wildest adventure of your life? Fantastic—welcome aboard!

And hello, fiery Aries! Pragmatic Taurus! Clever Gemini! Gentle Cancer!

Greetings, vibrant Leo! Thoughtful Virgo! Elegant Libra!

Salutations, strategic Capricorn! Innovative Aquarius! Supernatural Pisces! I love you all!

No matter what zodiac sign the Sun occupied at your exact moment of birth, you're here for a reason. And—believe it or not—the mystical compass that led you here actually transcends the zodiac. No matter what your birth chart looks like, the fact that you're reading this right now confirms a powerful, metaphysical truth: you're right where you need to be.

Although I'm an astrologer, and this book is about astrology, *This Is Your Destiny* is not structured around the zodiac. But wait—an astrology book *sans* zodiac?! Wtf? How is that even possible? Don't worry, there's a method to the madness. While the astrological archetypes are extremely important, this book is not a survey on the twelve zodiac signs. The reason for this is quite simple: **Every person *is* the entire zodiac.**

The zodiac is an invisible, 360° band that contains twelve parts (the zodiac signs[6]) across the ecliptic, which encompasses both the northern and southern hemispheres. Of course, at any given moment, only six zodiac signs will be visible by looking up (the other half are beneath our feet, on the other side of the planet)—but our birth charts factor in the *entire* sky, both above and below. Personal astrology contains *all* the zodiac signs, which means that even if you don't have a planet in a specific zodiac sign, you embody the wisdom of the whole cosmos.

You see, we astrologers don't *actually* reduce people to their Sun sign[7]—the Sun is an important star, but it's only one celestial body in the sky. In order to understand the full expanse of your individuality, we analyze the entire birth chart. Your astrological blueprint is structured around dozens upon dozens of planets and points, their corresponding geometry exposing the unique tension and harmony that makes you . . . well, you. Likewise, for the purposes of this particular journey, there's no reason to get caught up in the astrological jargon.

I want you to *feel*. I want you to *think*. I want you to *create*. I hope the stories and techniques and wisdom I've collected through my cosmic travels will broaden your vantage even further, projecting you deep into space and self—because these are, of course, one and the same.

HOW TO CREATE YOUR DESTINY

Astrology and manifestation changed my life. But don't just take it from me—I've worked with thousands of individuals in my private practice and watched my clients move from passive participants to active creators, using their innate truths to reach their highest potential. The relationship is, of course, reciprocal: my clients have also taught me new ways the universe can be expanded. This book is the physical manifestation of many years spent working with self and others on the astral plane.

Astral plane. Perhaps you've heard this term thrown around by your favorite metaphysical practitioners. It sounds cool . . . but what does it actually mean? **The astral plane is a fancy way of describing the non-material dimension that exists adjacent to our physical world.** The physical world, by contrast, is defined by sensory reality. It's the bedroom walls we decorate with posters, the pavement we pound during our morning commute, and the itchy, watery eyes we dread during a seasonal allergy attack. It's our clothes, furniture, finances, calendars, jobs, and everything else that has tangible form. Simply, the physical world contains everything that currently *exists.*

But before things exist, they must be created. In a sense, the astral world is the "behind the scenes" to the physical domain. The astral plane is the dimension that contains all the thoughts, ideas, vibes, wants, wills, intentions, manifestations, spirits, and energies that ultimately *become* tangible things. **We cultivate within the astral plane and *actualize* in the physical world.**

So, when I say that I work with clients on the astral, it's

because astrology is a portal that enables us to transcend the physical world. We look at *both* what exists in the physical, as well as the etheric, non-material astral realm. *This Is Your Destiny* is an exploration of this practice, expanded in a way that anyone, anywhere, can apply to their current realities.

Working on the physical and astral requires courage. In order to manifest, it's imperative that you throw *everything* out on the table—yes, including those very scary skeletons that have been stashed away in your closet for way too long. You'll need to be honest, hold yourself accountable, and be willing to face the facts, no matter how painful or uncomfortable they may be. To achieve real, lasting results, there's no room for excuses.

Does that sound doable? Terrific! After all, that's why you're here—there are no coincidences.

THERE ARE NO COINCIDENCES

When you spend time in the astral plane, you quickly realize **there are no coincidences**. I've adopted this statement as a sort of catchphrase—and, in my virtual community, the Constellation Club, we call it TANC for short.

TANC can be identifying synchronicities, like spotting 11:11 on a clock or thinking about someone just as they send you a text message. TANC can exist on a moment-by-moment basis, but TANC can also be complex, unfolding over many years like a Rube Goldberg machine: one small, seemingly arbitrary experience launches a totally unexpected trajectory that—slowly but surely—transforms your entire reality.

You may experience TANC situations simultaneously, sequentially, or randomly. When it comes to TANC, there are no rules or quotas or fancy metrics. TANC is merely a recognition of life's interconnectivity—TANC is an easy way to describe the ineffable link between the tangible and intangible realms. In a way, TANC happenings are like clues scattered across the physical plane—daily reminders that we're all aligned on a spiritual level. By identifying your own TANC experiences, you can follow the magical, electrical current that runs through time and space, inviting you to experience life with a heightened level of self-awareness.

And look at that—you've just found your way to the very first activity in this book! TANC!

Right now, think of three TANC experiences that stand out to you. Perhaps you had a totally random song stuck in your head, and then—a few hours later—you heard it on the radio? Maybe you met your current boyfriend on a dating app, only to discover that you actually went to the same music festival in 2012? Or, perhaps you're *already* keeping a list of daily TANC encounters, and are pleasantly surprised that your very first activity in *This Is Your Destiny* is to perform the exact same exercise you practice independently? Yes, that would be very TANC!

Whether the TANC experiences are large or small, from the present moment or distant past, go ahead and jot them down (you can use a designated journal, the notes section on your phone, or even the margins of this book). You may not know why these particular examples are coming to mind but—trust me—there's a reason. By the time you finish this journey, you'll have created a dynamic loop that will *certainly* be very TANC. Think of this exercise as an energetic placeholder to signify your starting point. This marks the beginning!

GET WHAT YOU DESERVE

Listen, I didn't think astrology was going to change my life. I was just looking for a way to *make sense* of my life. By the time I was in my early twenties, all the years of destruction and denial had finally caught up with me. Not only was I beginning to cycle through the same toxic behavior that plagued my teens—eating disorders, drugs, harmful relationships—but I was also living an entirely fragmented reality. I would, quite literally, tell different people different stories about who I was, where I worked, and even where I lived. I couldn't keep track of the narratives, and it became increasingly challenging to differentiate fact from fabrication. I was ripped into so many pieces that only the vast, incomprehensible language of the cosmos could *possibly* explain my reality.

But that's what makes astrology so special: astrology honors your full and complete truth. There's no need to truncate yourself—you literally have the entire universe to spread out. When projected onto the cosmos, you have permission to take up as much space as you need, visualizing yourself through a celestial context: an ever-expanding universe filled with infinite comets and planets and galaxies. So, the next time you gaze into a dark sky and marvel at the endless sea of twinkling stars, remember that you're looking into a mirror. **Fundamentally, astrology is a practice of self-love.**

Now, here's something you should know: I *despise* motivational décor. Personally, I find *nothing* inspiring about a throw pillow that tells me to LIVE IN THE NOW or DANCE LIKE NO ONE IS WATCHING. My disdain for this aesthetic also allowed me to keep the concept of "self-love" at arm's length. Simply, 'twas not my vibe.

But—looking back—it's possible that the very reason I had

reduced "self-love" to material objects is because I didn't know how to embody this concept in a more authentic way. You see, I didn't treat myself very kindly. Like, at all. I was unhappy with the way I looked, sounded, behaved, emoted, communicated. I scrutinized, nitpicked, and ridiculed every single thing about myself; trust that there was *truly* no stone left unturned. All in all, I think it's safe to say that I hated myself.

I justified this self-loathing through (what I perceived to be) "logic." I "knew" that all of my problems would be alleviated as soon as I was prettier, skinnier, wealthier, cooler, whatever. I believed that—in order to live my "best life"—I needed to be the "best me." And I imagined that I would *certainly* love this idealized version of myself but, until I reached those goals, the me I confronted each day in the mirror—that is, the *real* me—was undeserving of love.

I genuinely believed I *wasn't good enough* to give myself love. So I punished myself: Standing in a full-length mirror, I'd use a thick marker to circle every imperfection on my body like surgeons do before liposuction. *This is why you're miserable*, I'd whisper to my reflection. I'd calorie count, starve through self-inflicted fasting, and—when I couldn't resist temptation—shove two fingers down my throat to regurgitate whatever "indulgence" I'd consumed. I'd run for miles in the sweltering sun, intentionally dehydrated, with the goal of collapsing on the pavement, because only then would I *truly* know that I completed a full workout. I'd let older men—sometimes married older men—objectify me to fulfill their own delusional fantasies. And, to top it all off, I was horribly ashamed of my behavior, which only fueled further self-loathing. *You're disgusting, there's no way anyone could ever love you after what you've done.*

Although these examples are specific to my narrative, after

speaking with thousands of individuals over the years, I can confirm that self-loathing is more ubiquitous than many realize. The truth is that we, as humans, are more inclined to prove ourselves *right* than *wrong*. Informed by our own feedback loops, our internal experience mirrors our external experience and vice versa.

Perhaps you've already seen this play out. At some point, you may have found yourself *feeling* defeated, and your real-life circumstances seemed to validate your misery. For instance, if you believe you're "doomed to be alone forever," you'll often see this reinforced by your dating experiences. Perhaps every single person you meet vanishes after six weeks . . . or your lovers are constantly cheating on you . . . or you've been catfished on the dating apps twelve too many times. Whatever the circumstances may be, your romantic anxieties will play out in your reality, seemingly *proving* your hypothesis.

✖

Generally speaking, your life emulates what you *believe* your life should be, which means that—in order to shift your narrative from self-loathing to self-love—change needs to begin internally, within the astral realm, before it's realized in the physical domain.

And you are, right now, on the edge of transformation. Yes, you're still in the first few pages, but by the end of this book, you'll have acquired all the tools you need to cultivate the life you're actually excited to live—the one you *know* you deserve. But it's important to remember that real, lasting evolution doesn't happen overnight. It's the culmination of many dozens of choices, both large and small, that compound into profound metamorphosis.

Growth is painful, messy, and rarely linear. One step forward may be followed by three giant tumbles backward . . . along with slipping on a banana peel, knocking over a can of paint, and falling on your ass with a stubbed toe and a metal bucket on your head. Classic cartoon shit. But it will be worth it. I can assure you that the journey to self-actualization isn't only going to bring forth new opportunities, it will change the way you experience *being alive.*

Before we proceed, I need you to make a promise. Don't worry—it's nothing creepy. This is an agreement with yourself: **you must believe that you deserve to live your best life.**

Now, I'm not asking you to have a sudden, *artificial* revelation. Don't expect this promise to be the "eureka moment" that miraculously cures all your ailments, insecurities, and doubts. That would be totally inauthentic. I'm simply asking that you *accept* yourself as both whole and worthy as you are at this exact, present moment.

And, just to be clear, I'm not referring to the *idealized* you. Or the *mythological* you. Or the *aspirational* you. Frankly, I don't give a fuck about the Facetune-Photoshop-CGI version of yourself. I want you to embrace the real, honest you—the 360° you, as depicted in your birth chart, symbolized through the signs and planets and stars. The you who appears "together," but is actually falling apart. The you who's cranky, chaotic, dehydrated, and exhausted. The you who keeps slipping into the same shitty relationships. The you who struggles with boundaries. Complicated, contradictory, and completely unique. That's the you who deserves to live a truly extraordinary life.

The very things that drive you crazy about yourself are the same qualities that make you beautifully multidimensional—they're critical parts of your whole. When you accept yourself as complete (and completely worthy), even the parts of your person who previously hid, shamed, criticized, or scrutinized, become worthy of recognition. Astrology invites you to let all your truths exist in one place—against the backdrop of the ineffable cosmos, you have the space to be both neat and sloppy, sophisticated and belligerent, courageous and petrified.

At this moment, you don't need to change anything about yourself or your circumstances. You don't need to quit your job. Or break up with your lover. Or tell your alcoholic grandfather to fuck off. You don't need to fluff any pillows or wash any dishes or sweep any more secrets under the rug. Whatever adjustments need to be made will be approached slowly, thoughtfully, and intentionally— we'll get to those eventually, in the coming chapters.

Right now, simply observe. Acknowledge your life—all your truths—without judgement. Let your wholeness rise to the surface. Note your triumphs, failures, frustrations, and delights. This might feel scary or uncomfortable, so hold space for that, too. Know that nothing is static. The planets are always in motion and everything is constantly changing. And you, too, can transform your world. You have the ability to recalibrate or modify anything that will enable you to live a more exciting, inspiring, empowering life. And you don't need to wait until you're "better" to seek those opportunities— you're worthy of abundance, fulfillment, and joy *right now*. This is your narrative—and you deserve to write a fucking *incredible* story.

Using the wisdom of astrology, you're about to cultivate a bad-ass, supercharged, ultra-powerful manifestation practice that will quite literally expand your universe. Here's how it works: each chapter of the book addresses a specific area of life and— through stories and exercises—you'll shift your perspective, offering new vantages for you to identify your most authentic truths. Just like the zodiac itself, the chapters' lessons are cumulative, so as you press forward, you'll continue unearthing veracity in unexpected places. Since this will all be happening in real time, I suspect that—by the time you finish this book—you'll already be in the midst of an extraordinary transformation, perhaps even a full-blown metamorphosis as guided through unabashed authenticity.

Honestly, the formula is pretty simple: astrology fuels self-awareness, and self-awareness is the portal to self-love, and self-love is the gateway to your destiny. When you embrace your worth, there is no distinction between your dreams and your reality, so anything you desire can *become* your truth. And this is the essence of manifestation.

But what actually is *manifestation*? And how the hell does it even *work*? These are all great (and important) questions—and that's exactly why I decided to open a restaurant.

And look at that. Your table is ready.

WELCOME TO THE MANIFESTATION CAFÉ

Bonjour, mes amis! Welcome to the Manifestation Café! Today's special is . . . literally anything you want.

Now, what would you like to order? The soup? Excellent choice! I'll alert the chef.

Five minutes later. Here you are, *mes chéris!* The soup—just as you desired! *Bon appétit!*

Well, that was fun! But maybe you're wondering what the fuck just happened. Why did we just restaurant role-play? Did you just accidentally stumble upon some *Ratatouille* fan fiction? No—don't worry. It's nothing like that.

Generally speaking, the act of "manifesting" is extremely straightforward. In order to transfer energy (hopes, dreams, goals, desires, ideas, etc.) from the immaterial world into real life, you must create a bridge between the physical and astral planes. (We've already defined these terms, but here's a quick refresher: the physical plane is tangible reality, while the astral plane is the energetic "behind the scenes.") But, because manifestation isn't taught in school, the concept of moving fluidly between two parallel dimensions can feel a bit far-fetched. Metaphor is a terrific tool to help simplify esoteric principles. And, to help us understand manifestation, we'll visualize the process as a restaurant. The Manifestation Café.

As a customer at the Manifestation Café, you're located in the "front of the house"—the area of the restaurant that accommodates the public. The front of the house defines the look and feel of the establishment: it creates an ambiance, denotes the theme, and hosts the guests. In fact, because customers only interact with this area of the restaurant, the front of the house is what most patrons visualize as the entire restaurant. Likewise, in our metaphor, this section of the Manifestation Café represents the physical realm: it's all that exists within the tangible world. It's our perception of "real life."

But there's more to the Manifestation Café than the public-facing dining room. There's actually a whole other space, which—although invisible to guests—plays an integral role in the restaurant's core operations. Once a customer places their order, the server's next task is to deliver the request to the kitchen—an area known as the "back of the house." Unbeknownst to the customer, this kicks off a completely separate, albeit corresponding, series of events.

The meal is prepared through an intricate, systematic process. Everything moves like clockwork—with chefs and line cooks chopping, carving, seasoning—turning the customer's *desire* into something *real*: their meal. When the food's ready, the plate is transported again from the back of the house (symbolizing the astral plane) to the front of the house (the physical plane), for the customer to enjoy.

Indeed, our beloved, allegorical Manifestation Café isn't just famous for its exquisite décor—that's just one aspect of the restaurant. Ultimately, what makes the Manifestation Café special is its delicious, mouthwatering cuisine: five-star edible fare prepared in-house. So, although customers don't interact with the kitchen, this domain actually fuels the entire establishment. *It's where the magick happens!* Without this hidden realm, the Manifestation Café isn't even a real restaurant, it's merely a stage designed to *simulate* a restaurant. No substance, all façade.

I don't expect you to be blown away by this rudimentary description of a restaurant workflow. However, I've found this to be a very helpful way to visualize how these parallel dimensions operate both independently and collectively. Just as the entire restaurant is built on the communication between the front of the house and the back of the house, our manifestation practice is also structured around the exchange between the physical realm and the astral plane.

As an earthly being, you're situated in the tangible dimension. Your *energy,* on the other hand, is a product of the astral plane. Energy is yet another ambiguous spiritual buzzword—but essentially, it describes the infinite invisible forces that animate reality. Your personal energy is much like the universe: vast, profound, and ever-expansive. Energy is generated through intentions, desires, hopes, frustrations, fear, anger, sexuality, adoration, love, guilt, shame—energy is everything you feel, exude, contain, observe, direct, process, experience. Energy is everything.

In fact, energy is so broad and comprehensive that it can

feel a bit overwhelming—if energy is *all-encompassing,* how can you effectively work with it? The daunting nature of energy is one of the reasons that it's so much more comfortable operating within the physical plane than the astral dimension. But, in order to manifest, it's imperative that you create solid connections within both the physical and etheric dimensions.

As we continue forward, you'll become increasing familiar with both of these spheres of existence. While the physical plane will always be a bit more accessible (you are, after all, a physical being), one of the best ways to access the astral is by strengthening your imagination. Visualize stepping into your energetic space as if you're on a home improvement show—what does it look like? What does it contain? Is it ornate? Modest? Expensive? Is it a fixer-upper? Perhaps your astral dimension is totally empty. If you haven't spent any time exploring this etheric space, you may need to start from scratch. But that's also terrific—you're working with a blank canvas. Anything's possible!

Or maybe your psyche is filled to the brim with clutter: remnants of past, painful experiences. Hell, maybe all that dilapidated junk isn't even yours—maybe you inherited it from your parents. But your astral plane is *not* the family storage unit; it's an active, functional space that you access on a daily basis. So, if your energetic landscape looks like an episode of *Hoarders,* we're going to need to start clearing things out. I'm sorry, but nothing in the astral is ever "collecting dust." Every single day, your subconscious is quite literally *shaping* your reality. Psychic upkeep is critical!

Remember, the astral and physical dimensions are inextricably linked. You're constantly sending signals from one domain to the other and—just like at the Manifestation Café—"orders" are being churned out 24/7. There's no doubt that your real-life experiences directly impact your mood. For instance, if your lover breaks up with you randomly, you will certainly feel the effects on an emotional level. But it goes the other way, too: the astral manifests within the physical world. So, if you're convinced that you're destined to be a hopeless romantic forevermore, you will surely connect with lovers who substantiate that ideology.

What's important to note is that the physical and astral realms are linked in an infinite feedback loop. **Our psyche becomes our reality, and our reality becomes our psyche.** So it's no surprise that—when you're stuck in a toxic cycle—your worst nightmares can begin playing out in your everyday life.

Breaking a cycle isn't easy. In order to *disrupt* a destructive feedback loop, you must first identify the cycle, name it, and understand how it functions. Which thoughts trigger actions? Which actions trigger thoughts? Then, once you've discovered the link, you'll need to interrupt the flow by making an active, intentional change within *both* the physical and astral dimensions.

Although the physical realm may seem easier to access, it's important to note that this is a public space: we share this dimension with others, which mean this domain is shaped by external circumstances that exist beyond individual control. This is *precisely* why it's so important to fortify your relationship with the astral: unlike the tangible plane, the etheric dimension is private, entirely your own. Though you'll inevitably navigate others' insecurities and judgments and doubts in the physical plane, you can thoughtfully and intentionally *choose* to rid your psyche of rejections and blockages and fear—this realm should be inspiring, empowering, and magickal. What's more, it's within this domain that you can dream, imagine, and create the life you truly want to live.

Another thing to note: when working within the astral dimension, don't limit yourself with odds or probability. That's all stuff for the physical plane. Within the astral, you have the opportunity to explore your most expansive potential, embracing pipe dreams, lucky chances, and divine intervention. Let your psyche be the place of miracles—after all, this is *your* Manifestation Café. You're making the menu.

LET'S GET STARTED

The concept of the microcosm and macrocosm is pervasive across metaphysical practices. Designated containers (such as an individual's birth chart, a deck of tarot cards, or a bag of runes) hold the entire universe, which means no additional information or outside stimuli is needed for successful divination. Likewise, *This Is Your Destiny* abides by the same mystical philosophy. This book is intended to be read sequentially, because each chapter builds on the lessons detailed in the previous chapter.

You *already* have all the tools you need to live your best life; now, you just need to learn how to use them. Through compassionate self-awareness, you'll come face-to-face with your fears, insecurities, and vulnerabilities, breathing hope into your blockages and turning these energetic vacuums into active, dynamic psychic portals. You'll fortify your relationship with your intuition and discover that, anything (yes, anything!) is possible. Through fourteen supercharged manifestations, you'll learn how to generate desires on both the astral plane and within the physical world, creating an indestructible feedback loop that is guaranteed to change your life.

So, what are you waiting for? Let's get started!

✦

The cosmos
can guide you,
but they can't define you.

@alizakelly

TWO

KNOW THYSELF

"I'm lost, which path should I take?"

"How do I know if I'm making the right decision?"

"Should I take the risk?"

"Where do I go from here?"

ON IDENTITY

The first stop on our journey is a deep dive into the topic of self, which means exploring your core principles. The questions below are invitations, intended to spark reflection and curiosity. You can process them in a journal or in your mind's eye. Remember, there are no right or wrong answers. Let this exercise take you wherever you need to go.

- What does identity mean to me?
- In which ways has my identity changed over time?
- In which ways has my identity stayed the same?
- When did I last feel connected to my identity?
- When did I last feel removed from my identity?
- What helps me feel aligned with my identity?

IDENTITY MATTERS

"Well, what do *you* want, Katya?"

We were nearly halfway through our sixty-minute astrology session and Katya had painted a very vivid picture of her world: she grew up in Syracuse, New York, an only child in a two-parent household with a father (an accountant) and mother (a high school teacher). Born on September 14, 1995 at 4:12 P.M., Katya is a Virgo Sun with a Taurus Moon and Capricorn Rising. Triple Earth—we love to see it.

For as long as she could remember, Katya's parents encouraged her to pursue a corporate track—her father believed that working in business, for a large Fortune 500 company, would guarantee both stability and prosperity. Katya was an excellent student in high school and, when she was accepted into her first-choice college—New York University—she was elated. It was more expensive than her parents had hoped, but she assured them that, with a (practical) degree from a prestigious school, she would *certainly* be recruited by a top-tier consulting firm, like Deloitte or McKinsey, and have no problem finding steady employment. In fact, she was so confident, she was *sure* she would be able to pay her family back within just a few years after graduation. Her parents were soothed by Katya's dedication and agreed that NYU was the best choice.

During the winter of her sophomore year, she met her now boyfriend, Dylan, in one of her elective classes. They had an instant connection.

"He's a Cancer." Katya laughed. "Does that mean we're compatible?"

"Here's the thing," I explained, "the signs Cancer and Virgo are *technically* considered complimentary, but compatibility isn't just based on the Sun signs. We would need to calculate Dylan's entire birth chart—and *then,* we would need to see how *your chart* is impacted by Dylan's chart, and how *Dylan's chart* is impacted by your chart. Compatibility is always a two-way street."

"Yes," she said, "that makes sense." She didn't have Dylan's time of birth, but she explained how he grew up in an extremely affluent area of New Jersey. His childhood home was practically a mansion; Dylan's father was super successful (though she's still not sure what he *actually* does)—and, although Dylan doesn't see his father often, he has a close relationship with his mother, who Katya describes as "kind of superficial, but nice."

"Anyway," Katya explained, "I booked this session because I'm feeling lost and I'm not sure what to do." She had graduated NYU in May, and now it was October and she *still* didn't have a job. She didn't want to go back home to Syracuse ("It's way too far from the city"), so she was temporarily living at Dylan's family home in New Jersey until she could get her own apartment ("Ideally in the East Village or Williamsburg"). Both Dylan *and* Dylan's mother were encouraging Katya to explore opportunities in digital marketing, but Katya's parents were pressuring her to pursue a more traditional path.

"My dad is telling me I should just come home and get a job at this big pharmaceutical company upstate." Katya paused. "Should I just do that?"

My eyes darted across Katya's birth chart, which was brightly illuminated on my smudged computer screen. Sure, astrology can be used to derive a simple "yes or no" answer[8]—but after speaking with her for almost thirty minutes, it was clear that the *last* thing Katya needed was another person telling her what to do without taking into consideration Katya's *own* perspective. As an astrologer, my job is to offer cosmic insight custom-tailored to each client's unique circumstances.[9] In this case, I felt compelled to help Katya strategize for herself.

"Well, what do *you* want, Katya?"

After a short pause, Katya emitted a gentle, nervous laugh, "Actually, I don't remember the last time I really thought about that."

I wasn't surprised by Katya's answer. After all, she'd scheduled her appointment because she needed help navigating this particularly tricky crossroad. But, through our dialogue, I realized that the issue wasn't the job search—that was just a symptom of a much larger problem. Fundamentally, Katya had disconnected from her core truth: her identity.

I frequently discuss the topic of selfhood with my clients. Through traditional astrology, identity is most commonly associated with the Sun, the vibrant star located at the center of our solar system. This is also quite literal: the Sun exists to shine, so naturally, its warm radiance translates to raw confidence. **In the birth chart, this Luminary[10] is associated with ego, identity, and sense of self.**

Of course—from our perspective here on Earth—the Sun goes through its own transformation each and every day. Slowly at first, the Sun gains momentum as it rises over the east. As it climbs higher, the Sun becomes increasingly powerful (stronger, brighter, hotter), finally reaching its apex at midday (the *medium coeli*[11]). Just like Mufasa says to Simba in *The Lion King* (1994), everything the light touches is the Sun's kingdom—and, as the Sun hovers overhead—the entire landscape is enveloped by its powerful solar rays. After the Sun's dramatic crescendo, it begins to descend, dipping lower and lower until it finally disappears behind the western horizon, marking the culmination of its daily reign and the beginning of night (the Moon's domain).

Committed to its stunning performance, we can depend on the Sun's daily theatrics. But this solar showcase is also seasonal:

the Sun exudes a very different energy in the early morning than it does in midafternoon when it demands undivided attention like a diva in the spotlight. The Sun's platform isn't nearly as expansive in the winter as it is in the summer, which awards the Sun extended time onstage.

Accordingly, astrologers interpret the Sun in a birth chart based on a variety of factors, including its physical position in the sky, the zodiac sign it occupies (which, in Western Tropical Astrology, corresponds with the four seasons), as well as the aspects[12] it makes to other planets. All of these details provide critical insight about someone's identity and sense of self, along with potential obstacles and challenges. For instance, Katya's Sun in Virgo is located in the Eighth House, the area of the chart associated with transformation, intimacy, and inheritance (both financial and emotional). Katya's Sun and Venus (the planet representing values) are conjunct (close together), indicating that she's influenced by the way others perceive her alleged "worth." What's more, Katya's Virgo Sun is locked in a tense power struggle with her natal Saturn in Pisces (they're exactly opposite at 21°), indicating that Saturnine themes (narratives involving men, father figures, patriarchal systems, along with topics relating to work and fiduciary responsibilities) are at odds with her individual identity.

But this Sun-Saturn opposition isn't the problem—in fact, planetary aspects are *never* causal forces. **Astrology doesn't *make* things happen, astrology illuminates what already exists.** To visualize this, imagine a simple wall clock as it strikes six o'clock. The clock didn't *cause* the time to be six o'clock, it simply *reflects* what's occurring in reality. Likewise, the hard Saturn aspect to Katya's Sun isn't *fueling* this internal tension, it's simply defining the existing experience. And, when we add additional hands to the clock—a twenty-eight-day hand signified by the Moon, a 365-day hand represented by the Sun, a twelve-year hand symbolized by Jupiter, and so on and so forth—we can visualize time on a much larger scale. Indeed, astrology is just another way to observe cycles folding and unfolding.

Accordingly, the Sun's daily performance is a reminder that life is defined through movement. Every day, you're constantly adjusting, refining, and perfecting your perception of self as you rise, radiate, and set with the Sun. As you flow in and out of personal cycles, you'll explore different ideologies, modify your preferences, and tweak your tastes. All this in 24 hours? It's truly extraordinary.

And, just as the Sun sits in the center of our solar system, this *entire* book is really centered around identity because, fundamentally, astrology is a tool to deepen self-understanding, self-compassion, and self-love. As you continue forward, peeling back the layers of personal truth, I encourage you to proceed with curious compassion—after all, your discoveries aren't always going to be easy. Whether you're dredging up old memories, diving headfirst into painful emotions, or simply acknowledging mounting malaise, life is hard. But the only way you can use astrology to live your best life is by allowing your realities—good, bad, and ugly—to exist in broad daylight. **Like the Sun, you deserve to shine.**

✳

Earlier in our session, Katya offhandedly referred to herself as "deeply loyal." This made total sense—in fact, this self-descriptor aligned *perfectly* with my birth chart analysis. When I asked if Katya had *ever* disagreed with her parents, she said no—she always adhered to their rules.

"I love my parents," Katya explained. "and I respect them."

"Totally," I responded, "but is it disrespectful to advocate for yourself?"

As if I'd tapped her funny bone with a rubber hammer, Katya's nervous laughter reflex fired off: "I don't know—these are tough questions!"

During our late afternoon astrology session, the Sun was beginning to set, and Katya—living on her boyfriend's parents' New Jersey estate—began questioning her status quo. Katya had built her life around pleasing others. Perhaps, when she was a child, Katya was praised for mirroring her parents? Or, perhaps she was punished for disagreeing? We could surely uncover the narrative through additional conversations and birth chart exploration, but regardless of the backstory, Katya's coordinates were clear: she had lost touch with herself.

There was, of course, no reason to point any fingers or place any blame. It's likely that everyone in Katya's life *genuinely* wants her to succeed without ulterior motives. The fundamental issue is that Katya's world had expanded and personal choices could no longer be defined by her parents alone. Now, Katya was also influenced by her boyfriend and his family who— Katya mentioned—"may very well become [her] in-laws." In other words, Katya had even *more* important individuals to impress. And, with so many contrasting perspectives, how could she possibly keep everyone happy?

"Listen, it doesn't matter what anyone *wants* you to do," I said stoically—my Capricorn Rising making an appearance. "You need to focus on what *you* want. And, Katya, you can change your mind—you're not signing a binding agreement. But, right now, your homework is reconnecting with your intuition, your passion, and your internal compass. This is a practice in making your own decisions."

I know this is easier said than done. The hard truth is that Katya had spent her entire life accommodating others. She didn't know how to make independent choices, let alone prioritize her needs over others' expectations. Indeed, in order for Katya to embrace autonomy, she was going to have to start from scratch. By working on both the physical (external) and astral (internal) dimensions, Katya needed to manifest a sense of self.

Some readers may totally connect with Katya's narrative. In fact, many of us have a hard time cultivating identity *independently* from our social expectations. It's easier to "stick to the script" and play our "role" (in the case of Katya, the "good daughter") than take risks that challenge these external perceptions. **But people-pleasing is a short-term solution that creates long-term problems: by defining your value through others' standards, not only will you abandon your unique journey, you will also become vulnerable to toxic dynamics.** Energy vampires (individuals who leave you feeling depleted, drained, and/or fragmented) can smell vulnerability from a mile away—so if you continue to find yourself in manipulative relationships with hyper-controlling partners, check in with your symbolic Sun to make sure you're shining for yourself . . . and not for anyone else.

But other readers may be eye-rolling at Katya's tale. After all, Katya's "obstacles" are certainly imbued with privilege—she has a college education from an expensive private university, a loving boyfriend, supportive parents, and—in the absence of a job—has found herself cozied up in some *seriously* cushy dwellings. *Boo-hoo* Katya . . . cry me a river.

If Katya's "challenging" story reads like a fairy tale, I totally get it. But that's exactly *why* Katya's narrative is so important: even in the *most* seemingly stable situations, we can easily lose touch with our identity. Accordingly, readers who have endured objectively harder circumstances (especially those exposed to prolonged traumas, such as hostile childhood environments, abusive partnerships, or societal discrimination due to systemic racism and oppression) may find it increasingly difficult to align with their core truths. When you're in fight, flight, or freeze mode, you're fueled by survival, not self-actualization. For these individuals, the process of celebrating solar needs— what makes *you* shine—is of the utmost importance.

✖

Most of the time, individual growth is subtle—personal development is gentle, steady, and incremental. But consistency is *not* to be confused with stasis: indeed, life is defined through motion. Likewise, it should come as no surprise that—as soon as you start getting too comfortable and shift into auto-pilot—you're suddenly propelled into an unexpected, unprecedented growth that transforms virtually every aspect of your reality. TANC.

We now know that identity is ruled by the Sun, which means you must *always* remember that this *literal* superstar is an *actual* diva. Yes, the Sun rises and sets each day, but complacency implies disinterest. Let's get one thing perfectly clear: The Sun will *never* let its daily routine go stale—no fucking way! The Sun looks forward to each and every morning. Sunrise is a fresh start, a brand-new opportunity for this vivid luminary to show up and make an elaborate, unforgettable entrance. The sky is the Sun's stage, and this celestial body is always ready for the ol' razzle dazzle.

Like the cosmic star itself, your personal identity should radiate unapologetically. Of course, this doesn't mean you need to be bold or abrasive (or have a musical theater background, like I seem to be imposing on this personified Sun—whatever). It doesn't matter whether you identify as an introvert or extrovert, shy or outgoing, calm or hyper—frankly, you don't even *need* to define yourself. Who cares! **Each and every day, simply choose to be *you*.**

So, when it comes to manifesting your identity, embracing your personal glow is nonnegotiable. Considering that our ancient ancestors developed an extensive, intricate language to superimpose daily experiences onto the stars, it seems like our species understands this on a cellular level: humans are wired for "self-discovery." We've calibrated the sky to map our realities— astrology is basically a high-powered GPS.

But there's a catch. Before you can truly use astrology as a powerful tracking device to plot the fastest route to self-actualization, you need to know where you stand. I mean, you wouldn't expect Google Maps to deliver reliable directions without a signal, right? **The cosmos can guide you, but they can't define you.**

✠

Rarely, in astrology books, do we learn about the author. I think this is primarily for two reasons: (1) Since astrology is constantly being scrutinized by "skeptics," astrologers work twice as hard to legitimize their expertise, choosing to publish technical facts over anecdotal "fluff." (2) Astrologers know that, generally speaking, most people study the stars to learn more about themselves. Whether an astrologer is leading a client through a private session or writing an article about the twelve signs of the zodiac, we want to ensure that the material is engaging and relatable. I mean, let's be honest, when you book a session, you're interested in learning how a professional astrologer interprets *your* birth chart—it would be weird if the astrologer rambled on about themselves for sixty minutes!

In the first iteration of this book, I followed these unspoken rules. I focused on my clients and tried to maintain neutrality by crafting the voice of an omniscient narrator. Each time I attempted to write something personal, my index finger would find its way to the top right of my keyboard. *Delete, delete, delete.* That's way too much. I'm oversharing . . . this is too extreme . . . people will judge me.

But I came to realize that this internal conflict wasn't new. The truth is that when I first began studying astrology—almost ten years ago—I was *deeply* afraid of how others would perceive me. At that time, astrology still felt like it was reserved for eccentric great aunts who bathed in essential oils, wore excessive amounts of turquoise jewelry, and planned to retire in Santa Fe. And, while I appreciated that aesthetic, it was definitely not my personal vibe.

I wanted to be a professional. Or maybe I wanted to be an intellectual. Either way, I wanted to be taken seriously. It was one thing to study astrology privately or even share my interests with a few close confidants. But to reveal my passions *publicly* . . . well, that was a whole other story. I would be mocked—perhaps even ostracized—by mainstream society. If I started associating myself with astrology, there was no way I could ever just *waltz* back into a regular life. I mean, how could I ever secure a reputable job again? And what about love? Who would ever want to marry an astrologer?

Yes, I was afraid that working as an astrologer would prevent me living a normal life . . . but who was I kidding? I never wanted a normal life in the first place! In even my earliest childhood memories, I envisioned myself self-employed: crafting my own scheduling, fortifying my creativity, cultivating a career through extraordinary circumstances. Of course, I didn't know *exactly* what I would be doing—the vocation itself was always murky—but when I let my imagination run wild, my life felt vast and expansive and uniquely mine.

And, at the risk of sounding ungrateful, I was *never* satisfied by my regular jobs. Before becoming a full-time astrologer, I was an administrative assistant at a financial firm, personal assistant to an Upper East Side socialite, waitress at a fast-paced Hollywood restaurant, salesperson at a local computer shop, nanny to a family of five, barista at a college café, art dealer at a swanky contemporary art gallery, purveyor of a merch table at a music venue, and the front desk greeter at a fitness studio—along with countless other positions that have been lost in the sands of time. Some positions were hourly, others were salaried. But no matter where I worked or how much I was getting paid, I *always* felt like I was settling—like I was supposed to be doing something else. Looking back, this is proof that I wasn't unhappy with a *particular* job—I was unhappy with *every* job because I wasn't honoring my truth. I was insecure, fearful, and deeply doubted my potential. In short, I felt unworthy of living the life my heart desired, so I believed these were the only options available.

This also applied romantically. Once upon a time, I had a very specific type of romantic partner—I dated men who treated me like shit. The guys in my life couldn't even commit to dinner, let alone a serious relationship. Honestly, it's almost embarrassing to admit that I was worried an astrology title would make me "undatable," when it wouldn't have made a difference whether I was an astrologer, astronomer, or a fucking astronaut. The issue wasn't my cosmic passion, it was the fact that I gravitated toward men who didn't respect me. Why? Because I didn't respect *myself.* Is it a coincidence that, when I finally decided to be open about my adoration for astrology—talking about mystical and esoteric topics on our *very first date*—that I finally met a wonderful person who I'm thrilled to be with forever? Definitely not. TANC.

From my present-day vantage, it's clear that there was *never* a downside to embracing my truth through astrology. In fact,

I had nothing to lose and everything to gain. Although it may seem like simple arithmetic now, at the time, this realization was a complete and total mindfuck. **And that's because the issue was never** *really* **about embracing astrology—it was about embracing self-worth.** It was about moving beyond decades of pain and shame and doubt, giving myself full and complete permission to step away from others' expectations and be fulfilled by what I *actually* desired.

As you continue forward, consider the relationship between your Sun and Rising (also known as the Ascendant). The Ascendant is always located on the left-hand side of the wheel; on a normal clock, the Ascendant would occupy the nine o'clock position. The Ascendant shows us which zodiac sign was emerging over the eastern horizon at the exact moment of your birth. It's a sensitive spot that changes degree every two minutes, which is why astrologers are so adamant about accurate birth data.

I remember, in my early days of studying astrology, the Ascendant would often be described as "the mask you wear in public." And, while I understood this conceptually (even *before* masks became all the rage [no] thanks to COVID-19), it didn't quite make sense in application: Why was I wearing a mask in public? What does that mean? What did the Ascendant actually *do?*

It wasn't until I started exploring my friends' and relatives' charts that I began to understand how the Ascendant truly operates. **The Ascendant sets the stage for your reality—it's not the mask you wear, but rather, the genre of your life.** Those with a Leo Ascendant may move through a world that's dramatic, larger than life, and creatively charged, while those with a Pisces Ascendant experience reality as poetic, mysterious, and perhaps even a bit otherworldly. The Ascendant, which also establishes the First House (the area of your birth chart that represents your physical being) explains *why* your Sun needs to shine, your Moon needs to feel, your Mercury needs to communicate, and so on and so forth.

The Ascendant, in addition to your Sun, helps you understand *why* you are the way you are. What obstacles are you overcoming? What hills are you climbing? What thrills are you chasing? Of course, the Ascendant alone cannot explain your unique personhood—that's an incalculable amalgamation of planets and memories, society and circumstance. But, as it relates to self-actualization, the process of unpacking identity is invaluable. Simply put, in order to know where you stand, you need to know where you are. To apply this to your narrative, review Table 3 to prompt further reflection.

Honoring your truth is an act of self-love—an acknowledgement that you deserve to be happy and that you are worthy of living your best life. Now, I pass the torch to you. After all, this is your destiny.

IDENTITY REVIEW

- Defining identity is integral to self-actualization
- Prioritize your desires over others' expectations
- Practicing veracity will help you honor your truth
- The Ascendant reveals how you experience the world; the Sun symbolizes how you show up for that experience

MANIFESTATIONS FOR IDENTITY

Internal (Astral): Free-Association Spell

Life is fucking stressful—just staying afloat is a full-time job. But no matter how busy or exhausted you are, it's critical that you take time to check in with yourself. Because, let's be honest, in order to manifest *anything,* you need to know what you actually want in the first place. And you don't want your intentions to be piecemeal: your dreams are part of something greater—a reflection of the full, 360° scope that is your consciousness.

The first step to realigning with your identity is working on the astral—that is, the internal, psychic realm. Through my one-on-one work with clients, I've found that free-association exercises are a great way to explore your psyche. The **free-association spell** below is a personal meditation technique to help you get grounded, align your values, and cultivate a personal vocabulary that you can use to enhance your manifestation practice. In fact, the purpose of this exercise is to let your mind wander—invite your psyche to step into the driver's seat so that you can actively navigate the nooks and crannies of your subconscious realm. This is an opportunity to play. What happens when your imagination runs wild? Are there certain themes that surface? Unexpected discoveries? What will knee-jerk reactions reveal about your inner truths?

The below words are launching pads for your individual creativity. What does each phrase evoke? Perhaps another word? Or song? Or drawing? Or powerful breakthrough to amplify your self-discovery? You can jot your thoughts down in a notebook or sketchpad, or you can speak them out loud—either way, be sure to come up with your answers quickly; avoid the inclination to judge, scrutinize, or negotiate against yourself. The whole point of this exercise is to align with your core *independently* from outside influences, so do *not* overthink this. Most important, this manifestation is about opening your psyche, so have fun, get weird, and see what comes up.

Puppy *Example: Drawing of a paw print*
Chair *Example: Cushion, leopard print, gold, maximalism*

Acorn	Mustard
Glass	Disco
Coffee	Shadow
Alarm	Baby
Phone	Bubble
Computer	Zero
Return	Chandelier
Work	Hornet
Bounce	Trinket
Silver	Handshake
Climb	Love
Success	Noise
Balance	Effort
Wallet	Herb
Now	Purple
Roof	Commitment
Record	Forest
Cow	Reaction
Lost	Candle
Sneeze	Mice
Plant	Identity
Rotation	Sidewalk
Clock	Star
System	Yawn
Beer	Nurture
Icon	Slow
Check	Transparency
Art	Surf
Study	Vertical
Limit	Mirror
Safe	Self
Clean	

External (Physical): Dressing Your Truth

To bolster your manifestation practice, I recommend working on both the astral and physical planes. That way, there's a seamless connection between your internal experience and its external application. This is especially important as it pertains to identity—I mean, you want to make sure that the way you *feel* aligns with how others see you, right?

You know the old adage, "Dress for the job you want"? Well, this next manifestation expands on that concept, but applies it to every aspect of your life. In order to fully own your identity, practice **dressing your truth.**

How does it work? First, select a few of your core attributes that define your spirit (if you're not sure where to start, the free-association exercise should help kickstart some ideas). Then, head over to your wardrobe and find clothing items, shoes, jewelry, or accessories that capture the spirit of each trait. If you can't find any item to match one of your characteristic sensibilities, this is an indication that you need to connect with that energy more. Envelop yourself in it by—you guessed it!—treating yourself to a new item that expresses this quality. It doesn't need to be anything fancy; even a pair of cheap gas station sunglasses would suffice.

For example, let's say I describe myself as ambitious, playful, and sensitive (which I do). To convey my ambition, I chose my favorite vintage late 80s Vivienne Westwood blazer—a hand-me-down from my mother. I already wear this to 95 percent of meetings, so I make a point to intentionally associate this jacket with personal bad bitch energy. My playful nature, however, is best expressed through one of my bold, vibrant accessories: I chose these 5" long, gold skeleton earrings that I picked up for $10 at a Halloween store. They're spooky, silly, and—dare

I say—*kitschy chic*. Although it was a bit more challenging to find something that reflected my sensitivity (alerting me to the fact that I need to pay a bit more attention to this character trait), I finally settled on a gold locket that was a present for my fifth birthday. It always makes me emotional to think about my family before my parents divorced, so this necklace emanates nostalgic significance and reminds me that compassion is key.

Once you've selected your items, experiment with dressing your truth. With these pieces representing different aspects of your character, you can wear them whenever you'd like to amplify these corresponding character traits. Want to express resourcefulness to your supervisor at work? Or sensuality to your crush? Or don't-fuck-with-me vibes to your mother-in-law? Transform your closet into a costume trunk, filled with energetically charged pieces to help you express different dimensions of your identity within the physical realm.

Sure, clothes don't make the person—but they are a powerful way to communicate with the world. Likewise, instead of passively throwing items on with no intention, reimagine the act of "getting dressed" as a radical exercise in self-expression. The more comfortable you become wearing your truths, the more you'll be living them on a day-to-day basis. Remember, everything takes practice. When it comes to knowing yourself, the best way forward is complete and total immersion. At the intersection of *being* and *becoming*, this is your story!

✦

Money is an
emotional frequency.

@alizakelly

Before we begin this chapter, I want to clarify that—while money is an emotional frequency—it's also a real currency, and a violent weapon. Systemic racism is real. Class privilege is real. Pay inequality is real. And there are countless other ways money is used as a tool of oppression. Fundamentally, money is a symbol of power, and by throttling access to resources, money has—and continues to be—disproportionately distributed. This should not and cannot be ignored. Money manifestation does not exist within a vacuum. It must be acknowledged that ongoing oppression is ever-present within our historic and current realities. So, when you manifest individual abundance, be sure to expand your intention outward, manifesting financial liberation on the macro, as well. Be generous, be informed, and—especially for those who benefit from privilege—be willing to let go.

THREE

MONEY IS EMOTIONAL

"How can I change my relationship with money?"

"Why do I have such bad luck with finances?"

"What can I do to generate abundance?"

"When will I achieve financial prosperity?"

ON VALUE

Much to the dismay of financially minded stargazers who are captivated by the concept of fortune, the birth chart cannot predict whether you're going to be monetarily rich. But wait—don't roll your eyes just yet. After all, these are only the first few sentences of an *entire chapter* dedicated to money—the buck doesn't stop there (pun intended, obvs). The reason that astrology cannot foretell your financial status is because the concept of wealth is entirely subjective. As we'll discuss in greater detail, your perception of *personal* financial affluence is completely unique, calibrated specifically to match the infinite nuances that comprise your one-of-a-kind reality. Let's begin with a quick value survey, which can be explored in a journal or in your mind's eye.

- In what ways have my values changed over time?
- In what ways have my values stayed the same?
- When did I last feel as if my values were compromised?
- When did I last feel as if my values were celebrated?
- What helps me align with my values?

VALUE MATTERS

Courtney was born on July 24, 1986 at 12:49 A.M. in Fresno, California. And, when I asked Courtney what she wanted to explore during our session, she confidently shared that—at this moment—her primary focus was money. "So, um, can we talk about money?" Courtney queried.

"Oh hell yes we can talk about money! I *love* talking about money," I responded gleefully—and I meant it, too. After all, I'm a Capricorn Rising with a Second House Moon and an Eighth House stellium. (If you don't know what that means, don't worry—here's a quick translation: I fucking love talking about money[13].)

"Great! Well, I have a very shitty relationship with money."

Courtney proceeded to tell me that she's never been able to save more than a few hundred dollars at a time and, frankly, she couldn't remember the last time she wasn't living paycheck to paycheck. She's based in Los Angeles, which she knows is expensive, but everyone else seems to manage just fine. She wanted to know if there was something wrong with her? Was she cursed? Why was it so hard for her to generate abundance?

"Also," she continued, "I'm not a kid anymore." Courtney had just turned thirty-one, which meant *in addition* to her personal financial struggles, she now had to deal with all of her peers suddenly buying houses and investing in stocks and going on expensive vacations. "It's just making everything more overwhelming, feeling like I'm left out of these important life experiences."

At this point, however, I had to interject. "I hear you, Courtney, but just one thing. I know it may *look* like your peers are doing extremely well, but I can assure you that you will never *really* know what's going on in others' financial landscapes—not even your closest friends. You will *never* have enough information to gauge other people's resources, how they make money, and how they spend money, so don't even worry about comparing yourself to others. Just focus on you."

I asked her to please continue—but first, a quick clarifying question. "How *do* you make your money, Courtney?"

Well, she works as an administrative assistant for a real estate company. She actually started working at the firm three years ago—not because she was excited about the position, but because it offered a decent salary and health benefits.

"Honestly, Aliza, I'm so embarrassed because I literally took this stupid job because I was in a financial crisis and now, even with a salary, I'm in the exact same situation. In fact, I'm actually in a *worse* situation than when I started," Courtney lamented. "Seriously, am I cursed?"

"Of course not," I responded. "We just need to figure out what's going on. We need to identify the pattern. So, let me ask you this, Courtney: did you have career plans before accepting this job at the real estate company?"

"Yeah, I'm a photographer," she responded.

"Oh—amazing! So what happened when you pursued photography? Which types of gigs were you exploring?"

"I never actually pursued photography."

"Why not?"

"I mean, there's no money in photography."

Ding, ding, ding. This was the very clue I was hoping for—a distinctive stem we could trace to the root. Obviously, I wasn't relishing in her financial woes—I was thrilled because, thanks to her brave veracity, Courtney unknowingly revealed a *crucial* clue that exposed the multidimensionality of her financial concerns. Now, we could switch the conversation from *problem* to *solution*, putting Courtney on the fast track to sustainable prosperity.

For the diligent reader who has *no fucking idea* what just happened, allow me to explain.

From that brief back-and-forth, I received tons of important information about Courtney's financial landscape. First, I learned that her money issues were chronic—in other words, her "horrible relationship with money" wasn't triggered by an unexpected financial catastrophe (such as job loss or medical expenses) but, rather, indicative of her general status quo. In other words, Courtney's comfort zone *is* financial anxiety.

The fact that her financial issues were long-term—coupled with her (consistent) query about whether she's "cursed"—raised a few flags, but the real breakthrough was her offhand remark about her creative pursuit, photography. "There's no money in photography." *Eureka!* Not only was that a gross generalization (and also largely incorrect—there are plenty of ways to have a financially lucrative career as a photographer), but it also revealed Courtney's ailment: she was suffering from a bad case of scarcity thinking.

Scarcity thinking can be inherited (through family), acquired (through experience), or a combination of both. Scarcity thinking molds itself to the individual (in other words, it's specific to each person)—but once you know what to look for, it's pretty easy to identify: **scarcity thinking is a destructive feedback loop that sends a message to the universe that *limits* financial growth.**

If scarcity thinking sounds paradoxical . . . well, it is. In a way, scarcity thinking is a bit of a cruel joke. It's *not fair* that having financial anxiety stifles monetary opportunities! But this is why it's so important to visualize manifestation as an infinite loop: your psyche informs your reality and your reality informs your psyche.

To deepen our understanding of this concept, let's quickly swing by the Manifestation Café to demonstrate how scarcity thinking plays out within this metaphorical landscape. A guest (we'll call her Linda) enters the Manifestation Café, is seated by the host, and presented with the menu. Linda is very particular— she has a lot of dietary restrictions, so whenever she goes to a new restaurant, she's extremely concerned the kitchen is going to botch her meal. Since this is her first time at the Manifestation Café, Linda is expecting the worst—in fact, she's *confident* that they'll end up making a mistake. So, when she places her order with the server, she speaks primarily in negatives, detailing what she *doesn't want*: "I'll take this breakfast dish, but I don't like eggs, I can't eat meat, I'm gluten intolerant, and I got sick the last time I ate strawberries, so please tell the kitchen to be careful."

The server nods, although she isn't quite sure *what* Linda actually wants to eat. Normally, the server would try to clarify a confusing order—but Linda is sending out some serious "I'm-about-to-write-a-scathing-Yelp-review" vibes, so the server doesn't want to inadvertenly make the situation worse. She jots down Linda's "order" (which is really a bunch of items Linda *doesn't* want) and heads to the back of the house to inform the kitchen.

As expected, the cooks are equally confused. "Um, but the breakfast dish *is* an egg-based dish—are you *sure* she wants to order this?"

"Yes," the server sighs, "but just . . . no eggs. Or meat. Or gluten. Or strawberries."

Annoyed, the kitchen does their best to abide by Linda's fragmented guidelines, but, because the chefs are unsure what Linda even *wants* in the first place, the dish also contains no seasoning, no spices, no garnishes, and definitely *no* zest. It's lack-luster, uninspired, and extremely bland. When the dish is ready and delivered to Linda's table, Linda immediately notices the sad assortment of ingredients on her plate.

Linda frowns.

"This *is* what you wanted, right?" the server asks nervously, "we made sure to avoid anything you can't consume."

Well, this depressing dish is definitely *not* what Linda was hoping to enjoy—but technically, there were no mistakes. It was *exactly* what she ordered.

"Yes," Linda bemoans, "I suppose so."

And what does this story demonstrate? As depicted at the Manifestation Café, there's an inextricable link between your external world (that is, what's "actually" happening) and your psychic dimension (your internal, energetic reality). Linda was expecting to be dissatisfied with her meal, which catalyzed a series of events that ultimately led to a unappetizing breakfast.

And, in an almost identical fashion, my client Courtney is "placing orders" with the universe, just like allegorical Linda, by giving instructions built around anxiety, distrust, and limitations. Even in our session, Courtney outlined all the reasons she *repels* money: she has a horrible relationship with finances, she can't save, she's *never* saved, Los Angeles is expensive, photography isn't lucrative, she's cursed, and so on and so forth. The truth is that Courtney offered countless reasons she struggled with money . . . but virtually no reasons why she should receive it.

So let's get one thing straight: you're not struggling with money because you buy coffee. I repeat—you're not struggling with money because you buy coffee. I'm sorry to say, but your barista cannot be blamed for your financial woes. And *I know* your weird relative on Facebook is constantly posting about how "overpriced lattes" and "avocado toast" are making Millennials and Gen Z go broke—but you can tell your dear aunt Karen that I *guarantee* the wealthiest people are drinking designer espressos, enjoying avocado-based meals, and *still* amassing wealth.

So, if it's not the food or beverages, what could cause monetary issues? Astrologically, there are quite a few different planets associated with money. In traditional astrology, for instance, the Benefics (Venus and Jupiter) symbolize values and abundance, respectively. But wealth isn't currency alone. In fact, the concept of abundance has more to do with your emotional perspective than your bank account balance. **Likewise, chronic financial issues are best expressed through moonlight— money is a lunar matter.**

In the previous chapter, we explored the Sun's daily performance and how—from a cosmic perspective—this radiant superstar symbolizes identity. But when the Sun takes its final bow and disappears beneath the horizon for a well-earned slumber, it passes the torch to the other Luminary: the Moon.

Sure, you can sometimes spot the Moon during the daytime . . . but why would you want to? Against the backdrop of a clear blue sky, the Moon's vague outline seems awkward and exposed: honestly, spotting the Moon before sunset feels like opening the bathroom door on someone—*oh my goodness, I didn't know anyone was in there, I'm so sorry*—it's mutually embarrassing.

Indeed, this mysterious celestial satellite prefers the velvety darkness—it's at home in the night sky, among the stars and planets and swirling galaxies. This is TANC, because the Moon's astrological responsibilities are best suited for private introspection performed in the shadows. Reflecting the Sun's radiant glow, the Moon asks us how we *feel* about the external realities: how are you emotionally processing your day-to-day experiences? **Symbolizing the internal world, the Moon represents sensitivities, intuition, and nurture.**

Just like the Sun, the Moon is also extremely reliable—this Luminary also rises and sets each and every day. But while the Sun's behavior shifts on a seasonal basis, the Moon's mood is *constantly* in flux. Not only do we observe the Moon's sprint across the sky approximately thirteen times faster than the Sun's daily journey, but the Moon also moves through its own unique cycle, expanding and retracting against the magnificent celestial curtain. Every twenty-eight days, the Moon aligns with the Sun and disappears into shadow, marking the New Moon. Then, over the next two weeks, the celestial satellite waxes—moving from a crescent, to a quarter, to a gibbous—until it reaches maximum visibility during the Full Moon phase, directly opposing the Sun. Then, the Moon begins to wane, retracing its steps—from gibbous, to quarter, to crescent—as it glides back into the darkness.

While the Sun has a mythological association with the Hero's Journey, the Moon has long been linked to feminine energy, specifically the role of the mother. In *The Luminaries: The Psychology of the Sun and Moon in the Horoscope* by Liz Greene and Howard Sasportas, the authors describe the Moon as representing our basic needs for safety and survival, which they refer to as "lunar foods."

Since money is a symbol of security, our relationship with finances is reflected within our natal lunar placement. As with every celestial body, there are many variables that influence an astrologer's interpretation of the Moon, including its physical location, zodiac sign, and prominent aspects. In Courtney's birth chart, the Moon (situated in watery, psychic Pisces) is locked in two very tense aspects: a direct opposition to Venus (the planet of values) in Virgo, and a harsh square to Saturn (the planet of restrictions) in Sagittarius. These placements could certainly suggest lunar ailments—perhaps her chronic financial troubles are the result of emotional malnourishment?

Money, like the Moon, is malleable and fluid and irregular—it mimics the Moon's fluctuations, expanding and contracting on a daily basis. Some readers may be surprised by the correlation between money—hard, permanent, and serious—with the sensitive, shape-shifting nature of the Moon. After all, the idea of money as anything other than "logical" contradicts the way we're often taught to interact with currency, but money is far from rational. Much like our own emotional landscapes, money is volatile and messy and complicated. What's more, our *understanding* of money is derived entirely from what it symbolizes—an extension of the psychic, astral plane.

For example, consider one hundred dollars. What does one hundred dollars mean to you? How often do you spend one hundred dollars? Now, imagine how a ten-year-old would react to one hundred dollars. Or how a multi-millionaire would respond to the same amount. What about a mother who's raising four children on her own? Or a street performer in a subway station? Or a Wall Street broker transferring funds from one account to another? Although the technical "value" of one hundred dollars remains unchanged, the significance is entirely contextual: we need to understand the who, what, where, when, and why to make sense of *true* value.

Your individual relationship with money is shaped by both your physical (external) and astral (internal) realities. By establishing the connection between money and the Moon, you have the ability to transform your relationship with finances. How? Just like the Moon, your financial situation is *never* static: motion creates waves, and likewise, new opportunities. By reframing money as an extension of your *emotional* being—as opposed to an entity that functions entirely separately from your psychic, subconscious needs—you can *experiment* with the way you get and receive funds. Embracing money as fluid, flexible, and adaptable—mirroring your sensitivities—it enables you to create new monetary possibilities that may exist outside your established perception of resources. By infusing your consciousness—and, subsequently, your wallet—with creativity, play, and joy, you'll systematically shift your internal rhetoric from lack to abundance.

I should mention that I relate to Courtney's experience. Like so many of us, I also struggle with scarcity thinking—and with good reason. A few years ago, I could barely keep my bank account above zero (though, to be fair, I was also thousands of dollars in credit card debt, so really, I didn't have any money at all). Of course, that didn't happen overnight. Just like the fictional character, Mike Campbell, says in Ernest Hemingway's 1924 classic *The Sun Also Rises*, I went bankrupt two ways, "gradually and then suddenly." Iconic.

In my family—on my mother's side—relatives speak of great fortunes and great losses. Every story follows a similar pattern: there *once* was money and then *something* happened and *poof*. All gone. The stories are vague, mysterious, and often pose more questions than answers.

Both of my maternal grandparents were the descendants of Ashkenazi Jews who came to New York through Ellis Island in the late 1800s. My grandfather's side—originally from Belarus—settled in downtown Manhattan, while my grandmother's family—from Hungary and Poland—migrated to the Bronx. My great-grandfather, Papa Louie, allegedly owned a successful bar and grill in the Lower East Side, but, one day, he cut my grandfather out of the business to appease a greedy partner and . . . *poof*. All gone. Uptown, my grandmother's father, Papa Benny, worked in Harlem in an unknown business that apparently did well, but after the Great Depression . . . *poof*. All gone.

In a way, these tales of financial tragedy feel mythological, almost Romanov in nature. To *lose* all your money implies that there *was* money—and, when you're dodging bill collectors like mosquitos—ineffable lore provides invaluable comfort. But these "fall from grace" stories didn't end with my great-grandparents. My grandparents' money was *also* swallowed by gambling (in elementary school, I spent most weekends at my grandfather's favorite tri-state casinos), impulsive purchases, and unreliable accountants.

Unfortunately, it didn't end there, either. I watched this narrative continue down the line, as my mother also spiraled into financial destitution. Yes, there were indisputable hardships. There was the unnecessarily expensive divorce that didn't just break up my parents' marriage, but also their business partnership. My parents, both music industry professionals, were originally connected through their publisher to team up in songwriting and producing. There was also my mother's devastating cancer diagnosis that catalyzed years of surgery and radiation and chemotherapy and exorbitant medical bills. And then there were things that transcended my mother's immediate circumstances, like the music industry's failure to regulate file sharing software like Napster and LimeWire, which took an unprecedented financial toll on artists and creatives.

I can verify that all of these things *really* happened—there were specific, undeniable reasons that, by the time I was ten, my mother qualified for low-income housing. I understood why we shopped for groceries at stores that accepted food stamps, and why—when I applied to college—I was able to receive federal grants eligible to students from financially disadvantaged backgrounds. It all made sense, but there was a deep fissure that separated my real life and the romantic, fabled past simply titled "early childhood."

My relationship with money was built on folklore, and likewise, I felt like a modern-day Anastasia, with recurring financial collapse as an inherited family curse. What the fuck even *happened* in the shtetl two hundred years ago? Why was it impossible for my family to accumulate wealth? Who knows—but, by the by the time I was in my twenties, the cycle was already gaining momentum . . . only this time, it was my story.

I had virtually no idea how to make, manage, save, or even *discuss* finances. I was terrified of losing everything before I even had anything to lose, which meant I accepted jobs based solely on my *perception* of value, which was—as I'm sure you could imagine—not a very reliable method. In 2013, two years after graduating college and working as an administrative assistant, I moved to Los Angeles to pursue a career in the art world, an industry that seemed . . . well, expensive. As if money was a perfume, my financial philosophy was to situate myself "near" affluence, so that maybe I could pick up some of the aroma, too. And, at that time, I believed *any* income was better than no income, so I accepted an annual salary of $30,000 and opened a credit card (which generously offered 0% APR for the first twelve months—what a deal!) to pay for what I couldn't afford.

Although the writing was on the wall, I didn't have the financial literacy to know that making below minimum wage and supporting yourself on credit was a recipe for disaster. I saw that plastic card as supplemental income, and for a few months, my life was relatively normal.

Los Angeles is home to Hollywood—a strange noun that is part ideological concept, part geographic neighborhood, and part entertainment industry. In 2013, Los Angeles put another concept-neighborhood-business on the map: Silicon Beach. Silicon Beach was Los Angeles' response to the multibillion-dollar tech industry that had already shifted the landscape of Northern California. It modeled itself after the "Founder/God" archetype established by Steve Jobs and Mark Zuckerberg—but it was younger, brattier, and sexier. That was, at least, the idea.

Just a few months after I moved to Los Angeles, twenty-three-year-old Evan Spiegel turned down Mark Zuckerberg's $3 billion offer to buy Snapchat, a "power move" that sent tingles down every movie executive's spine. Now—sprinkled with entertainment business stardust—talent agencies became tech incubators, film producers transformed into venture capitalists, and movie sets morphed into venues for start-ups' hedonistic launch parties (known as "activations"). There were ice luges and T-shirt launchers and celebrity cameos—and, if all of this seems way too bizarre to be real, remember this is the cultural moment that created Billy McFarland's iconic Fyre Festival scam: ego, access, and disgusting amounts of money.

I, however, was broke. Like, really broke. But since I didn't know the difference between $30,000 and $300,000, I decided to step into the ring—in 2014, my best friend from college and I launched Align, an astrology dating app. Building and destroying Align was a wild, bizarre, and truly life-changing experience. I hope that, one day, Helen and I will have an opportunity to share those stories together. Until then, however, this is what I'll say about Align: we started an astrology company at a very special time, when extremely affluent individuals were taking big risks on innovative, unexpected companies. Unfortunately, Align wasn't one of them.

Since the venture capitalists never invested in Align, we were never able to commemorate our success with ice luges or T-shirt launchers or celebrity endorsements—let alone have the resources to pay ourselves. I had rent and bills and mounting debt (the introductory 0% APR eventually expired, eventually giving way to a horrifying 29% APR), so in 2015, I left my low-paying gallery job for another low-paying job (albeit with slightly more flexible hours so I could continue building Align), working as a waitress at a now-defunct restaurant on the Sunset Strip. I was a horrible server and, after six months, I got fired. And then I collected unemployment. And then, when that ran out, I started selling my clothes on Craigslist.

The Align situation was dire: by 2016, it was clear that no "angel investor" was going to miraculously swoop in and save our astrology dating app. And, when we finally decided to walk away from Align in August 2016, I had even less money in my bank account than I did before we started. I was cobbling together minimum payments from odd jobs and focus groups, tracking every single penny I spent and avoiding buying anything I could potentially find for free (special shout-out to my former roommate, Katie, who generously gifted me her collection of hotel toiletries, providing me with a stockpile of tiny shampoo and conditioner bottles so that I didn't need to buy hair products). After three years in Los Angeles, I sold all my earthly belongings on Facebook Marketplace, and scrounged up enough cash for a one-way ticket back to New York. I distinctly remember those last few hours in Los Angeles: sitting on my apartment complex's patio, lighting a cigarette, and checking my bank balance on my phone: $38.74. There was nothing more.

For the sake of sounding totally corny, it was that moment—on that patio, with that cigarette, looking at that bank balance—I experienced a strange, unexpected emotional breakthrough. There was something oddly cathartic about reaching rock bottom: a feeling of calm acceptance, gentle surrender.

You see, I was absolutely petrified of running out of money. The idea of going broke felt so destabilizing to my Second House (the area of the chart related to material possessions, including currency) Pisces Moon, but truthfully, I never had financial stability in the first place. I had been living paycheck to paycheck, making barely enough money to pay my bills. I was *always* on the edge of an overdraft fee. For years, I had been moving through a feedback loop fueled solely by anxiety, but the fear never generated change. And, for whatever reason, on September 13, 2016—the day I moved back to New York—I finally realized that living in this constant state of worry was not only taking a toll on my psyche, but it was also doing virtually *nothing* to improve my financial situation. The only way I was going to break this vicious cycle was by generating change from within.

Although my astrology dating app had failed, by that point, I had spent three years studying the cosmos on a daily basis. I was familiar with the ins-and-outs of the birth chart, including my Moon. With so many of my personal planets positioned across the Second and Eighth House axis, it became clear that my emotional experiences were actually *realized* through my relationship with money, which meant *all* my insecurities that compounded over the years were expressed through these financial blockages.

This self-awareness allowed me to expand my vantage. It became clear that, in order to improve my financial circumstances, I need to build my confidence, which required a twofold approach. First, I had to acknowledge the harsh truth of my current situation. I had to admit that I wasn't just broke circumstantially, I was *chronically* broke—but this veracity enabled me to rebuild trust with myself. What's more, my budding astrology practice taught me that time was not chronological, but rather cyclical, which meant that even if my reality *felt* static, I was still in motion. My *current* situation didn't need to be my *forever* situation.

Likewise, the "curse" on my family wasn't financial loss, but rather, financial lament. Indeed, each generation was inheriting the story that—one day—some catastrophic event would create monetary ruin. And this Romanov-inspired "fall from grace" narrative wasn't just a distant threat; it was a realistic *expectation*. There was no future, there was no present—all energy was directed toward the past. Likewise, the second step to rebuilding my confidence and improving my financial situation was to do the exact *opposite* of my ancestors: I needed to look forward, toward the monetary possibilities that had yet to materialize.

I also discovered that there was no reason to shame myself for being broke: not only was that unhelpful, it was actually quite destructive—I needed to build *up* my confidence, not beat myself down. So I began meeting myself with gentle compassion. I acknowledged that, although I had tried very hard, it wasn't working, and thus, I needed to change my approach. Yes, all I had was $38.74 and, obviously, I needed to make money. So, when I arrived in New York, I continued to support myself through odd jobs, temporary positions, and seasonal gigs, but my entire attitude had shifted. My grip was looser. My vision was clearer. My perspective had changed. This was the bedrock to building an abundance-based mentality.

Of course, my new abundance-based mentality wasn't immediately reflected in my bank account—that would be both completely unrealistic and entirely impossible. Through 2017, I worked on turning up my financial thermostat (a technique I'll describe in the manifestation exercises at the end of this chapter) while simultaneously fortifying my self-worth independently from money.

Then, in June 2017, a childhood friend invited me to lead a Full Moon workshop at her new studio space on the Bowery—my first paid astrology gig. Tickets were $12 and that night, after we split the profits. I made $60. Sure, it wasn't much, but thanks to my rapidly transforming relationship with money, I knew that the actual dollar amount was relatively inconsequential. After all, money *always* ebbs and flows so, rather than focus exclusively on the monetary earnings, I reflected on the extraordinary magic of that experience. Holy shit, I just got paid to host an astrology *workshop*.

Propped on throw pillows on the floor of a downtown loft, I spoke to a group of strangers about the stars and planets and cycles. I was thrilled to publicly share all the wisdom I had been quietly accruing for the last several years: I talked about the Moon, its astrological symbolism, and how to locate the Full Moon phase within a birth chart. We concluded the evening with a Full Moon manifestation exercise and, after the workshop ended, I was shocked to see people lingering to ask more questions: *Will you be back to host another class? Can I book a private session? Are you available to read charts at my birthday party next month?*

This response was totally unexpected and absolutely extraordinary. To be paid in any capacity to practice astrology was a complete dream come true, so I exchanged emails with the guests and followed up the very next day. From there, things started moving very quickly: I was scheduling in-person client sessions, booking corporate astrology events, and even an editor at *Allure* magazine reached out about a new weekly horoscope column—my first paid writing gig. By September 2017, I was already making more money as an astrologer than through my hourly temp gig. In late October, my friend and fellow astrologer Jessica Lanyadoo introduced me to an editor at Simon & Schuster who was interested in publishing a fun, playful astrology book. I drafted an outline and wrote a sample chapter for what would eventually become *The Mixology of Astrology* and, in December 2017, signed my first book contract. With a manuscript in the works, I made the scary—yet tremendously exciting—decision to commit myself to a full-time astrology practice, establishing an LLC and business account shortly thereafter. I never looked back.

Fast-forward to the present: my life is abundant. I've paid off my credit card debt. I have a savings account and a retirement fund and financial goals. I'm in the position to comfortably support my family—my mother and grandmother—as needed. I donate to organizations frequently, and, when I hear that someone is in a tight spot, offer resources to help. I give generously, and receive abundantly. Fundamentally, I know that, so long as I continue to honor money's organic wax and wane, my finances will flow in a way that is supportive and sustainable. I'm profoundly grateful to have a healthy, bountiful relationship with money, a true 180° from where I was not *that* long ago.

But the most important thing to note is that my relationship with money didn't change in the physical realm—the real work was entirely within the astral dimension. **Money is an emotional frequency, which means your relationship with finances is cultivated in the psyche.** Likewise, if you're interested in transforming your economic circumstances, it's essential that you actively, thoughtfully, and honestly reflect on your present-day situation. Perhaps scarcity thinking is rooted in your family line, or lack mentality from previous financial traumas is preventing you from moving forward, or deepseated insecurities are blocking you from reaching your fullest potential? And, since change is inevitable, there are countless opportunities to flip the script. This is one of them—let's do it!

VALUE REVIEW

- Money is innately fluid
- Your individual relationship with money is a reflection of values, which are subjective, contextual, and deeply personal
- Values are both inherited and acquired, but they can always be transformed
- The Moon reflects your emotional security, offering insight into your relationship with values

MANIFESTATIONS FOR VALUE

One quick note: Regular reflection is a critical component within any money manifestation practice. The questions outlined in the beginning of this chapter are great prompts to jumpstart exploration, but—because money is an emotional frequency—it's vital that you have a safe space to process the past, plan your future, and purge any anxieties that may cause energetic blockages. I suggest investing in a journal to be used exclusively for your money manifestation practice.

Internal (Astral): Turn Up Your Thermostat

One of the best ways to generate abundance is by checking the settings on your thermostat. No, not the one on your wall. The one in your psyche.

You see, we all have a financial "comfort zone." At some point, it's likely you've subconsciously settled on a number that feels rewarding, yet realistic. This number may be a dollar amount in your bank account, an hourly rate, or even your annual salary. Take a moment to reflect on that figure: what's your personal "sweet spot?" That number indicates where you've set your financial thermostat.

When you're below that number, you're cold. You feel underpaid, undervalued, and financially strapped. Of course, you want to get back to your comfort zone as quickly as possible, so you throw on a few layers, hustle extra hard, and figure out how to return to your status quo. During this time, you may scale back your spending, experiment with different budgeting philosophies, or even apply for higher paying positions. After all, you're focused on reaching that target number—you hate being uncomfortable!

"Money manifestation" is super trendy right now—and why

wouldn't it be? But what happens when you actually *receive* the capital you manifested? What happens if it's hundreds, thousands, or hundreds of thousands of dollars out of range? Is it getting hot in here?

When you've *exceeded* your financial status quo, behavior changes radically. Of course it's exciting to have *more* money—but this extra cash feels like a surplus. Now, you might even start sweating. Overheated, you strip down and spend the overflow. On one hand, you're spending because you have the money to do so—maybe you've been wanting to refurnish your living room for a while, and this is the perfect opportunity! But that's not *all* that's going on: with more resources than normal, you're also spending because you're outside your comfort zone. Simply put, you're purging the excess.

We see this phenomenon often with people who suddenly come into a lot of money: overnight sensations, trust fund recipients, lottery winners. When the temperature on our financial thermostat goes up too quickly, we get overwhelmed and frantically spend back down to normalcy. Likewise, when you're in unfamiliar territory, you'll find yourself returning to your factory setting—or even dipping beneath it—to return to a more comfortable temperature. In cruel irony, manifesting too quickly and without the proper resources can actually *create* financial hardship.

So, while I'm all about money manifestation in theory, I'm also extremely wary of the get-rich-quick schemes I see popping up all over social media. Sure, you can have more—but if you're not ready to receive it in a sustainable way, you can lose more than you ever imagined. And that sucks! Likewise, the money manifestation that I recommend to clients (and that I personally practice, as well) is called **turn up your thermostat.** Fundamentally, the way this works is by consciously and intentionally increasing your "comfort zone." By turning up your thermostat's dial slowly, thoughtfully, and—*ahem*—responsibly, you won't get overheated by the additional resources you manifest. In fact, whatever you generate will always feel like the perfect temperature: Not too hot, not too cold. Absolutely just right.

To perform this exercise, note the current settings on your financial thermometer. Perhaps it's the number in your bank account, or your weekly paycheck, or even what you have tucked away beneath your mattress. What is your current comfort zone? Be honest, and jot it down in a designated journal (or, if you haven't yet invested in a notebook, the margins of this book will certainly suffice).

Next, we'll need to adjust the dial to a slightly higher number. If you're not sure how much to increase, know that small intervals are absolutely fine. Remember, this isn't a gimmick—this is a way to *permanently* amplify your abundance to ensure you can cultivate a long-term prosperity that's healthy, sustainable, and realistic.

When I first began practicing this exercise, my thermometer was set to $1000. Back in 2017, maintaining a thousand dollars in my bank account seemed realistic—because I had done it before—and also comforting; $1000 meant I could handle an emergency if absolutely necessary. However, I would get anxious if I even went *slightly* below $1000, and—if I had above that amount—I would feel *too* fancy, and end up "treating myself" back down to my comfort zone.

So, when I first turned up the thermometer, I ruminated on how much I should increase the temperature. I thought about adjusting to $2000—but could I imagine having that in my bank account? No, at the time, that felt *way* too unrealistic. Actually, that seemed like an impossible amount of money. So I went back down a bit—could I imagine having $1500 in my bank account? Yes, I could. That seemed approachable. So I turned my thermostat up to $1500.

I visualized logging into my bank's website, pulling up my account, and seeing $1500. I imagined the way that number would look in a sans-serif font and how comforted I would feel knowing that I would definitely be able to pay my bills. So, with this new temperature in mind, I began shifting the way I was interacting with money on a daily basis. Instead of focusing on how much I was *spending* (a nervous habit that amplified my scarcity mentality), I made a point to emphasize how much I was *saving*.

Eventually, I reached $1500 in my bank account, and as soon as I hit that number, I made a point to press that figure into my psyche as my new normal. I wrote it down in my journal, decorating the page with dollar signs and hearts and stars, like I was a twelve-year-old doodling about her crush. I actively maintained that temperature, and soon enough, anything even *slightly* below that figure felt unsettling—which was truly wild to experience, since just a few weeks prior, anything over $1000 made me feel like a rock star. So, when I felt ready, I adjusted it again—this time to $2000. And then to $2500. And then, as I started to feel more comfortable with this method, I began adjusting for larger increments: $3500, $5000, $8000 . . .

This process takes time. It won't happen overnight—it literally can't and, actually, that's the point. This manifestation, to be performed in the astral, is about increasing your tolerance so you can receive not only abundance, but also financial longevity. Ultimately, you'll set the pace of this manifestation based on what's realistic for your circumstances. Remember that the first few adjustments will be uncomfortable—yes, you might even get a little sweaty working your way up to these new temperatures. But trust that this technique is *extraordi-*

narily powerful—stick with it, and it will *truly* change your relationship with money forever. I should know; I'm living proof of its efficacy!

External (Physical): Keeping it Fluid

As you're dialing up your thermometer in the astral, you can also expedite abundance by working in the physical plane. But, believe it or not, this manifestation actually requires spending money. That's right—this technique is all about **keeping it fluid.**

Not so fast there, champ. Before you whip out that credit card and start buying unnecessary shit on the Internet, it should be noted that this exercise doesn't just apply to *any* ol' purchase. This technique asks that you send resources where they're *actually* needed.

Within this chapter, we learned that money isn't static; like the Moon, it always waxes and wanes. In the late-stage capitalist society that serves as the backdrop to this book, we're often advised to "wall off" our resources: we have *ownership* of our cash and the best way to increase net worth is by never, *ever* letting it go anywhere but back into our *own* pockets. In the words of Gordon Gekko in *Wall Street* (1987), "greed is good."

While any comprehensive financial plan will, of course, set funds aside to remain untouched (often designated for retirement or emergency situations), the money we interact with on a regular basis is extremely fluid. Our balances wax and wane—and this is totally fine. In fact, it's organic: money, an emotional frequency, demands an energetic give-and-take.

Likewise, this manifestation technique mirrors money's natural undulation, inviting us to intentionally reflect money's innate movement in our individual financial habits. The act of keeping it fluid sends a message to the universe that you, too, are in flow and, therefore, a perfect recipient for expansive abundance.

For those readers who are in precarious financial situations, the idea of *giving* money can feel extremely intimidating—especially when you're just trying to scrounge together enough resources to get by. But let me fill you in on a little secret: even when you're struggling with money, you will *never* experience financial strain when you help others. Sure, you might feel that quick pang of anxiety because—let's be honest—it can be scary to loosen your grip and open your wallet. I totally get it. But helping others through generosity actually opens the door to new financial opportunities. In fact, it's one of the most powerful money manifestations you can perform.

So what makes it so special? You see, this act is performed in the physical world. It's neither internal nor reflective: you are quite literally redistributing resources. Giving money isn't a trade—you're not exchanging money for goods or services and, frankly, you shouldn't even inquire about where the money *goes* after you released it into the astral. After all, money is always borrowed, never owned. What this exercise *does*, however, is open a fruitful channel for abundance.

Ready for more good news? You can use this technique whenever you'd like to generate abundance. For instance, if you're about to receive a contract and you're hoping the offer is going to be generous, this is an excellent time to practice this manifestation technique. First, choose the recipient. It can be a personal connection (such as a friend or relative), nonprofit organization, crowdfunding campaign, or complete stranger. In this manifestation, there's no hierarchy of need—the only thing that matters is that you *want* them to receive the unexpected resources.

How much money should you give? There's a very simple formula to determine the correct amount: after you've selected the recipient, a number will pop into your head—this is an intuitive reaction. Most likely, you'll try to negotiate with yourself to lower the number ("a hundred dollars seems like a lot . . . seventy-five dollars is probably fine . . .) but here, commit to the amount you originally intuited. *Of course* this unsuspecting individual will be happy to receive anything—but that's not the point! That mysterious figure that arrived in your psyche is a hint from the universe, revealing the fastest way to open a financial portal. Yes, you may wince for a moment, but don't worry. That grimace will quickly evaporate . . . especially since your generosity will be exponentially rewarded.

If you send resources to someone you know personally and they ask you wtf is going on, you can respond with a sly "just because" or you can explain that it's part of your manifestation practice ("I'm keeping it fluid to generate financial abundance"). If they refuse to accept the money for whatever reason, you'll need to start the process over again with another recipient—but don't stress. That will happen occasionally. It's all part of keeping it fluid.

One very important thing to note is that you *cannot* put any stipulations on the gift. In other words, you cannot instruct the recipient on how to spend the money. By telling them what (or what not) to do with the funds, you are *still* claiming ownership of that capital and subsequently closing the feedback loop, as it becomes a one-to-one monetary transaction. Keeping it fluid means you are redirecting your resources, awarding the recipient full and complete autonomy. There's no problem if they want to tell *you* their plans, but you cannot decide on their behalf.

As soon as you practice this technique, you'll be stunned by its incredible efficacy. The best part? You never reach a limit! You can perform this manifestation *anytime* you want to create more resources for yourself—whether you're saving up for a big purchase, paying off credit card debt, or just need some extra spending cash. It can become part of your monthly (or weekly, or even daily) routine. Personally, I use this manifestation as frequently as possible. If even the *tiniest* seedling of a thought crosses my mind ("Oh, this person is trying to raise money for medical expenses . . ."), I immediately grab my wallet. Is it compulsive? Sure—but I fucking love money—both getting *and* giving. And, when you keep it fluid, the universe is inspired to keep it flowing. Onward and upward!

✦

Don't speculate,
communicate.

@alizakelly

FOUR

CULTIVATE YOUR CONNECTIONS

"How can I cut ties with a toxic relative?"

"Is this friendship worth keeping?"

"How will I meet my 'people'?"

"What can I do to improve this relationship?"

ON CONNECTION

Humans are social beings. Interpersonal connections—platonic and romantic—are a crucial part of our journey: our friends, family, classmates, and colleagues actually help us align with our truth, offering invaluable perspective on the road to self-actualization. But maintaining these relationships is challenging. In fact, because they can be so difficult to navigate, they're often omitted from healing narratives altogether, perpetuating the false narrative that strengthening individual consciousness is a solitary, independent experience. While I send sincere blessings to anyone who chooses to drop off the grid and find spirituality through reclusion, I believe that self-discovery is not achieved through isolation, but rather, through community. In this chapter, we'll explore the significance of relationships, as well as ways to improve interpersonal dynamics. But first, take a moment to check in with yourself in the present moment—these questions can be answered in a journal or through quiet meditation.

- When was the last time I checked in with my connections (existing relationships as well as past relationships)?
- In what ways have my interpersonal relationships changed over time?
- In what ways have my interpersonal relationships stayed the same?
- When did I last feel appreciated by a close colleague, classmate, friend, or relative?
- When did I last feel unappreciated by a close colleague, classmate, friend, or relative?
- What helps me deepen my connection with others?

CONNECTION MATTERS

Toward the end of our birth chart reading, I asked Sarah if there was anything else she wanted to address before we wrapped up. "Well, can the chart show interpersonal problems?" Sarah responded. "I have no idea what's going on, but recently, my entire life feels like a soap opera."

First, she explained, she got into an argument with her colleague, Jill. Sarah and Jill work together for a small, boutique interior design company. There are only five people in their office, and because Sarah and Jill were pretty close in age, they became fast friends. They saw each during the day, tagged each other in memes at night, and even grabbed brunch on weekends.

But, one day, something shifted. The company landed a new project with a swanky, high profile client and—almost immediately after the team began working—Jill's energy changed. Practically overnight, Jill became cold, disconnected, and even competitive. Sarah wondered what was going on, but didn't know how to bring it up. After all, Sarah didn't want to create an awkward work environment. Eventually, however, Sarah felt like she needed to protect herself, too, and started distancing herself from Jill.

Sarah—feeling snubbed by Jill's iciness—decided to pitch some new concepts to her boss. A few months earlier, she and Jill talked about exciting future projects over cocktails, but Sarah felt like these were ultimately *her* ideas. And, whatever, she didn't need Jill anyway. Of course, there are *no* secrets in a five-person office and Jill quickly found out that Sarah had excluded her from the conversation. Jill was furious. Sarah tried to backtrack and explain that Jill had actually hurt *her* feelings first, but Jill wouldn't hear it. At this point, rebuilding a friendship seemed totally out of the question. In fact, Sarah wasn't even sure how they could possibly continue to work together. What a nightmare.

As if that wasn't stressful enough, Sarah was *also* navigating serious tension with her mom. Two weeks prior, Sarah's mom was sick with the flu, and asked Sarah to pick up some groceries for her. But, unfortunately, Sarah was busy with work stuff—could she go the next day? Her mom said yes. So, Sarah went shopping on Saturday, but when she dropped the groceries off, her mom was *also* giving her the silent treatment. Sarah tried to find out what was wrong, but her mom refused to communicate. Sarah stormed out and, since then, they've barely spoken at all. But this lack of dialogue wasn't atypical for Sarah's mom. Sarah told me that her mother has always been cold and distant and, as Sarah put it, "only reaches out when she needs something."

But wait, there's more! The straw that *actually* broke the camel's back was when Sarah got into an argument with her husband, Ryan. Sarah and Ryan have been married for three years— generally, they got along quite well. But, over the past several weeks, Sarah had been totally consumed by all the Jill drama. Sarah admits that she complained to Ryan about it . . . *a lot*. Like, incessantly. Yes, it was basically all she talked about. But then, one day, Ryan just snapped. "Listen, I'm not your therapist. I don't want to hear about this work bullshit anymore!" Sarah was devastated.

"What does my chart say about all of this?" Sarah asked.

Astrologer Anne Ortelee has an amazing motto: "If it's in your heart, it's in your chart." In other words, whatever is happening in your life—either in the emotional or physical realm—will be mirrored in your birth chart. So, when we look at your birth chart along with transits (that is, the planets moving around the sky in real time), we can extract a deeper understanding about what's shaking down in your day-to-day reality.

The way planets connect with each other is called "aspects." Traditionally, we categorize aspects as either "good" (also called "soft") or "bad" ("hard"). Soft aspects mean that the planets get along swimmingly—they effortlessly support one another and amplify each other's best qualities. Hard aspects, on the other hand, create friction. The planets fundamentally disagree with each other, fueling frustration and discord.

Squares (planets meeting at exactly 90°) are often considered the *toughest* of the hard aspects (Table 4). Like the most intimidating ruffian shooting darts in the back of the motorcycle bar, squares are the meanest of the mean. Squares coincide with tension, and can often feel like getting elbow-jabbed in the stomach.

But there's more to squares than painful blows. Scientifically-minded readers may recall that, according to the laws of physics, pressure is defined as force applied at 90° right angles—and pressure always results in release. **Likewise, squares remind us that it's only through discomfort that we can activate our full potential.**

So what does a square look like in application? Squares are choosing the wrong major in college, only to discover your true calling after you've invested time and energy in the wrong classes. Squares are breaking up in the middle of a two-week vacation, only to find that you're *happier* enjoying a solo adventure. Squares are constantly disagreeing with an old friend, only to realize that you have the ability to break the cycle by firmly advocating for your needs.

I wasn't surprised to discover that Sarah's chart was riddled with squares—interpersonal relationships often show up through this aspect. Born on March 9, 1988, at 6:16 P.M. in Baltimore, Maryland, Sarah's Pisces Sun (conjunct the North Node, indicating she was born during an eclipse season) was locked in a tense aspect pattern known as a T-Square with her Virgo Ascendant–South Node conjunction and Gemini Chiron–Midheaven conjunction. Without even knowing the real-life scenarios that contextualize this T-Square, this aspect pattern made it clear that Sarah experiences her fair-share of conflict. This isn't necessarily a *bad thing*, however: in order to grow, we must be challenged, and one of the fastest ways to identify personal pain points is through our closest companions.

In fact, our relationships catalyze self-actualization; connections demand accountability. After all, you aren't a rogue asteroid hurtling through space—you're a shooting star sailing through a shower of like-minded meteors. Important relationships nudge you (and occasionally shove you) outside your comfort zone. They invite you to expand your reality, broaden your horizons, and align with the *collective consciousness*.

For those unfamiliar with this term, the collective consciousness is a fancy way of describing the psyche of the macro—the notion that you're part of something bigger than just yourself. The collective consciousness operates on a societal level:

it's through the collective consciousness that we experience humanitarian movements, fashion trends, and even political eras. But it also operates on an interpersonal level. The types of connections you cultivate with others inform your interests, ideas, and preferences. Accordingly, your closest bonds are actually gateways to understanding self *relative* to the external realm.

Suffice it to say, the symbolic significance of interpersonal dynamics can even transcend the relationship itself. Friends, family, colleagues, classmates, and even neighbors can be soulmates. These connections enable you to look at the world through a different lens, inspiring empathy, compassion, and understanding. Likewise, the term "soulmates" shouldn't just be reserved for romantic partners (we will, however, discuss matters of the heart later in this book). Sometimes, you're paired with a soulmate your entire life—you're inextricably linked as you orbit, hand in hand, through individual and shared cycles. But this is not the norm. In fact, most of our soulmates will not last a lifetime. Just as you're constantly growing and evolving, your relationships will transform, as well.

Soulmate bonds can last years, months, weeks, or even days. The length of the relationship doesn't necessarily indicate its impact. Connections move through states of activity (for instance, you may spend a lot of time with a friend when you're in the same city, but lose touch when you're farther apart), but if a relationship no longer sparks empathy and compassion it may have reached its apex.

But how can you tell which relationships have lost their luster, and which are continuing to thrive? And what can you do to improve strained dynamics? Sarah's threefold drama is a great way to explore different types of interpersonal struggles because Sarah's actually working through three *completely different* conflicts. Although Sarah is the common denominator, each relationship (Sarah to Jill, Sarah to her mom, Sarah to her husband) is unique. Likewise, each interpersonal conflict demands its own bespoke solution.

This also exposes something I encounter often when working one-on-one with clients: despite the fact that every relationship is one-of-a-kind, interpersonal bonds are often grouped together. It's easy to conflate dynamics—in many ways, it's how we interact with the world. We understand family "units" and meet friends in "groups." When speaking about multiple people, it makes sense to refer to the larger entity (for instance, my "high school friends," or "my father's family," or "my professional network"). While this is a useful tool for communicating, it's not how your interpersonal dynamics work on an *individual* level. No, your relationships are *specifically* between you and another person, *even* if that person exists within a specific greater social structure. Likewise, each connection needs to be considered as a one-on-one exchange.

Compounding relationships prevents you from understanding the nuances of each individual dynamic. Every person in your life has unique offerings that speak to hyper-specific lessons. And, even if some interpersonal connections overlap, the magic of an individual story is nestled within the details of a one-on-one relationship. Likewise, we need to be mindful of not just the role someone plays in our life (lover, friend, colleague, etc.), but also *how* the relationship developed in the first place. What's the genesis? What's the trajectory? What am I learning through this unique connection?

Now, I know some of you are thinking, *Aliza, that seems exhausting—do we *really* need to analyze each relationship individually?* And, well, it's a yes from me. In the same way that establishing your identity and defining your values are critical components of living your best life, thoroughly understanding the nuances of your interpersonal dynamics is *also* an essential component of the self-actualization process. Toxic dynamics can hold you back from reaching your highest potential, whereas supportive bonds can actually propel you forward. In order to determine how you're impacted by your relationships, each meaningful connection in your life needs to be explored carefully, thoughtfully, and compassionately.

In astrology, compatibility is often calculated through a technique known as "synastry." To visualize the interpersonal dynamics of two people, astrologers render synastry charts by overlaying birth charts, one on top of the other. To better understand the relationship between Sarah and Jill, for instance, we would calculate two synastry charts: One that reflects how Jill activates Sarah's chart, and another that reveals how Sarah illuminates Jill's chart (Plate 4, Plate 5).

With Sarah's chart in the center, we see Jill's Scorpio stellium primarily illuminates Sarah's Third House (representing peers, communication, and local affairs). Sarah's natal Moon is at 1° Sag-ittarius, while Jill's natal Moon and Uranus are 2° and 4° Sagittar-ius, respectively, suggesting a powerful connection between their individual and collective emotional worlds. Interestingly, as the Moon also reveals maternal influence, it's possible that Sarah and Jill have similar issues with their mothers. When we look at Jill's chart, Sarah's planets are sprawled across several houses, though this display makes it easier to notice that Sarah and Jill share the exact same Mars placement at 11° Capricorn. TANC.

The reason we analyze synastry charts side- by- side is because *all* relationships are a two- way street. Synastry serves as a re-minder that every relationship is an exchange. We often forget to consider the role *we* play in the other person's story, and syn-astry reminds us that relationships require reciprocity. How do you influence, impact, and guide others' journeys? Are you a positive, supportive influence? Do you give people space to show up as their best, truest self? Through astrology, we understand that every person is a complex, unique soul, with their own expectations, wants, and perceptions of reality. In that same vein, your best friend may satisfy *your* demands for comfort and stability—but how do you know you meet *their* needs?

The best way to explore the duality of any relationship is not through speculation, but through communication. Compassionate curiosity will help you establish an open dialogue with your companions, enabling you to explore the similarities and differences of your wants, needs, and expectations. **Remember, transparency, intimacy, and honesty shouldn't just be reserved for romantic partnerships—*any* notable relationship warrants conscious conversation**. But, if the idea of having a heart-to-heart dialogue with a friend or relative makes you uncomfortable, that *also* provides invaluable insight on the limitations of that bond. It's not about whether it's "good or bad"—this moral binary is *so* limiting—it's about accepting the *truth* of the relationship.

In astrology, Mercury is the planet of communication. Named after the Roman messenger god (Hermes in Greek mythology), Mercury governs expression, language, transportation, and all forms of transmission. As far as celestial bodies are concerned Mercury is definitely among the most popular—even folks with absolutely no interest in astrology know this planet for its infamous backward spin. Three or four times each year, Mercury pauses, pivots, and begins cruising in reverse, a notorious moonwalk known as "Mercury Retrograde" that's believed to cause miscommunications, malfunctions, and all types of technological meltdowns. Of course, Mercury doesn't *actually* go backward— this phenomenon is an optical illusion—and Mercury Retrograde doesn't *actually* wreak havoc; it's all just a matter of perspective.

In traditional astrology, Mercury plays an unusual role as neither a Malefic nor a Benefic, but rather, a fluid entity that shapeshifts depending on its company. In the birth chart, Mercury symbolizes language, expression, and the way information is both shared and received. Sarah's Mercury is positioned at 22° Aquarius, indicating that Sarah's communication style reflects the Aquarian qualities of intellectualism, innovation, and—yes— perhaps a bit of that signature aloofness. Unsurprisingly, Jill's Mercury meets Sarah's at almost *exact* square: With her Mercury at 21° Scorpio, Jill's expression is intuitive, deep, and protective. Further, while Sarah's Aquarius Mercury is focused on precedents that apply to the greater good, Jill's Scorpio Mercury is much more personal, prioritizing honest, intimate one-on-one connections above philosophical debate.

Looking at these charts, I would *image* that Jill's initial silence was due to private matters outside of work . . . but, of course, I couldn't know for sure, and neither could Sarah, *considering she didn't ask*. **The truth is that no matter how talented you are at astrology, tarot, or any divination practice for that matter, speculation will never be as effective as communication.** In fact, the entire conflict between Sarah and Jill could have been avoided though thoughtful discourse. When Sarah noticed Jill's energetic shift, a simple "hey, what's going on?" would have offered invaluable insight. Did Sarah do or say something hurtful? Was Jill feeling competitive about this new business venture? Maybe Jill needed a different type of emotional support, but didn't know how to ask for help? Without conversation, Sarah hypothesized, obsessed (inadvertently causing friction in her *own* marriage), and ultimately, lashed out. Unfortunately, by this point, honest communication isn't about clarification; it's about damage control. If Sarah wants to repair her relationship with Jill, she's going to need to lead with honest humility and apologize.

Even as we do our best to establish transparency, some of our most integral relationships will be far from ideal. It's quite common, especially in relationships between relatives, that interpersonal bonds will never meet your individual needs. We *hope* our loved ones will change, mature, or understand, but too many instances of recurring disappointments demonstrate that evolution isn't likely. Sometimes, we'll need to walk away from these bonds completely but—even more often—we'll choose to keep the person in our lives *despite* the frustrations.

Although these are some of the most challenging dynamics to manage, *accepting* the limitations of hampered relationships can actually *improve* the connection. Rather than grasping at straws, desperately trying to siphon support that doesn't exist, setting realistic expectations and establishing emotional boundaries enables you to accept the relationship in its true form. Let's be honest: if someone doesn't embrace the 360° version of you, there's no reason you need to give them 100% of your energy. Otherwise, you're just setting everyone—including yourself—up for failure. By *accepting* the relationship for exactly what it is, you give these complicated dynamics more breathing room, which actually opens them up for new possibilities, including growth.

During our session, Sarah explained that—no matter how hard she tries to improve her relationship with her mother—she always seems to reach a dead end. Her mother simply *cannot* provide the emotional support Sarah so desperately craves—and there's a profound sadness to that truth. But I explained to Sarah that she's built an entire life for herself *despite* her mother's limitations. So, although it's painful to admit, Sarah doesn't *actually* need her mother to be any different than she already is. Likewise, by acknowledging that her mother is incapable of particular types of affection, Sarah can begin to break up the stagnant heartbreak that compounded like plaque throughout her lifetime. By infusing veracity into her life, Sarah creates space for emotional discovery. What happens if—instead of waiting for her mother to change—Sarah actively chooses to approach the relationship differently? After all, we do not have control over others, but we can shift the way we, individually, move through the world and interact with others.

Dear reader, please know that you truly *don't* need to cycle through the same shitty circumstances over and over again. You have agency. You have options. You have free-will. So, by accepting the truth of a bond (no matter how challenging it may be), you're making the *decision* to acknowledge the entirety of the dynamic (the good, bad, and ugly), giving it permission to be exactly what it is. The implications of this are extraordinary: it will not only improve the troubled relationship, but it will also strengthen your self-identity, as well as your bonds with *every single person* in your life. Yup—I told you. Extraordinary.

In order to reach your highest potential, it's imperative that you practice total and complete veracity. When I began my self-actualization journey many years ago, I remember feeling like someone had injected me with truth serum, like I was Jim Carrey from *Liar Liar* (1997). After years of living in denial and falsities—desperate attempts to protect myself from exposing vulnerability—I suddenly couldn't stop being honest. I felt like a fire hydrant busted open on a street corner, gushing observations *no one* wanted and making a total and complete mess. *Clean up on aisle Aliza!*

Interestingly, my urge to tell the truth followed the collapse of my fragmented infrastructure: When I moved back to New York—broke, alone, defeated—all the facades I worked so hard to maintain were shattered. I could no longer pretend to be "together," and like the Tower card in a tarot deck, I was letting it fall apart. And for the first time ever—my realities flowed freely.

My confidence was building, my anxieties were reducing, my relationships were improving, and I was actually . . . having more fun? In a fairly short amount of time, opportunistic "friends" who only reached out to justify their own bad behavior, energy vampires, and toxic enablers began to vanish. In their place, authentic connections with people who challenge, support, encourage, and inspire me in genuine, sustainable ways.

What I didn't know at the time is that I was in the midst of experiencing a symbolic death and rebirth, and my newfound veracity was the symptom of a powerful metamorphosis best described as a "spiritual awakening." Although this term is frequently thrown around metaphysical communities, what *actually* happens during a spiritual awakening is rarely defined, which is why I didn't realize that the sudden compulsion to be honest meant my day-to-day reality was shifting from the inside out. But, in my work with clients over the years, I've discovered that you don't have to wait for your entire world to crumble in order to catalyze a spiritual awakening. **You can actually initiate a spiritual awakening through the simple— yet profoundly difficult—act of telling the truth.**

I shared these thoughts with Sarah in our session, leading with the no-bullshit yet deeply compassionate attitude that has become my signature style. Did I think Sarah was *lying* about her story? No—I'm sure Sarah's account of these interpersonal gymnastics genuinely reflected her perception of reality. But, as an astrologer, I'm an expert at spotting patterns and I couldn't help but notice the narrative's repletion: Sarah was afraid of communication.

One of the primordial rules when navigating interpersonal relationships is accepting that you cannot control others: Not what they do, not what they say, and not how they feel. Of course, this is easier said than done—especially for sensitive souls who want to absolve others' hurt, pain, and disappointment. But there's actually nothing kinder and more compassionate than supporting others' individual experiences *independently* from your influence. Practicing veracity means complete accountability for your individual journey—and recognizing others as solely responsible for their narratives, as well.

Cultivating meaningful connections is an extension of embodying your truth. Express your honest thoughts, feelings, wants, and desires, accepting that your friends and relatives are entitled to their own opinions and perspectives. Your closest companions may not always agree with your choices, just as you may not always agree with their decisions—and that's alright. As you strengthen your communication, remember that occasional tension within interpersonal dynamics is not only normal, but also extremely *important*. When in doubt, share what's on your mind: Why is the disagreement making you uncomfortable? What is your preferred method of exchanging information? What are your expectations for the bond? Yes, relationships are hard work—but that's exactly what makes them worthwhile!

CONNECTIONS REVIEW

- Each relationship is a completely unique entity that exists independently from all other bonds
- Squares are challenging aspects that enable us to uncover our full potential
- Interpersonal dynamics can be explored through synastry charts
- Mercury is the planet of communication, which offers insight into your unique expression

MANIFESTATIONS FOR CONNECTIONS

Internal (Astral): Reciprocity Table

We know that self-actualization is hard work. We know, for instance, that we *couldn't possibly* change our financial situation overnight. So why don't we spend more time reflecting on our interpersonal bonds? The hard truth is that we usually don't think twice about our existing relationships until something starts going wrong. Whether you're getting annoyed at someone—or someone is getting annoyed at *you*—tension often forces us to reassess our interpersonal dynamics. Unfortunately, even when we make thoughtful adjustments, it's easy for relationships to slip back to the old ways, propelling the same undesirable cycle forward.

Here's the deal: *do not—I repeat do not*—wait for disagreement to take a closer look at your bonds. Not only does this approach prolong unwanted behavior, furthering anger and frustration, but—if and when the tension is actually addressed—the relationship is "resolved" under artificial conditions. Everyone's on edge, so any changes implemented are in response to the *disagreement*, as opposed to the *dynamic* itself.

Often, when arguments occur, someone is reacting to an emotional imbalance. Likewise, it's important to remember that every dynamic is an energetic exchange: there's always a give-and-take. **So, the best way to nurture your existing relationships is to visualize this exchange by creating a reciprocity table.**

For an internal (that is, astral plane) manifestation, you should use the reciprocity table to explore all your important relationships. Don't forget, each relationship is unique and, therefore, you need to create reciprocity tables for *every* important relationship in your life—don't even *think* about trying to group people together!

To create a reciprocity table, grab a piece of paper or a clean page in your journal and draw a two-column table, with one column labeled "GIVE" and the other labeled "GET." (Also, you may want to write your companion's name on the top, so you can keep your reciprocity tables organized!) In the GIVE column, outline all of the things you bring to the relationship. Are you a great texter? Do you initiate plans? Do you offer thoughtful, supportive advice? Are you excellent at karaoke duets? Are you hospitable? Don't worry about whether your list sounds silly; as with all manifestation exercises, nonjudgmental honesty is paramount. Jot down whatever comes to mind—somewhere in your psyche you're already keeping tabs on all your contributions, so this is merely a place to put the observations that *already* exist.

Next, move over to the GET column. What do you receive from the relationship? Intellectual conversation? A shoulder to cry on? VIP access to your favorite music festival? Nonstop laughter? Again, take note of anything and everything that surfaces during this exercise. Not everything you receive needs to be "socially acceptable" either—if your co-worker is an amazing drinking buddy, write it down. If your Instagram influencer friend makes you look cool, write it down. Fundamentally, we want everything out on the (reciprocity) table. This is a private exercise, so don't worry, you won't need to share this with anyone.

The first time you practice this manifestation, I recommend completing two or three reciprocity tables back-to-back. Explore each relationship independently *before* reviewing your answers. Once you've evaluated each dynamic, compare and contrast the different tables. How are the bonds similar? How do they differ? Do you notice recurring themes or patterns? If so, where do they show up—the gives, the gets, or both?

Through this practice (both the creation and reflection), you'll dial up your self-awareness and become more thoughtfully connected to your interpersonal relationships. If a dynamic is off-balance, consider ways you can harmonize the bond. Do you need to give more? Less? Are you taking too much? Getting too little? Also, if you notice similar attributes across all relationships, reflect on that cycle. Are you seeking a particular type of connection? Does that dynamic mirror meaningful relations from childhood? Do you want to continue this pattern, or break up the narrative with new types of relationships?

Ideally, this manifestation should be performed as maintenance to ensure that you're consciously aligned within your relationships. This is an excellent practice for the monthly Full Moon, when the celestial satellite illuminates the night sky. During this lunation, we can see everything that is usually hidden beneath the shadows, so you have a unique opportunity to explore even the most complex interpersonal dynamics.

You may also perform this technique anytime you have the slightest inkling of trouble. If you're starting to get irritated by your friend, or if you feel like your friend is acting oddly, grab a pen and prepare your reciprocity table. Ultimately, this is an exercise in self-actualization—the more you understand your truth, including how you connect with others, the more easily you can align with the universe to create your destiny.

External (Physical): Tap Your Truth

Before we review the technique for the physical dimension, let me clarify how this connection-based manifestation works. We can only shift our own *individual* consciousness, and likewise, this exercise is designed for you, and you alone. Your friend, relative, or colleague does not need to participate in manifestation—you can successfully improve the dynamic by tapping into your autonomy.

But that doesn't mean that your companion is off the hook. Just because you're choosing to invest in yourself (and, subsequently, your interpersonal bonds) doesn't mean that the entire relationship falls on your shoulders. In fact, a mini-manifestation you can perform to generate transparency is *telling* your friend that you're in the midst of an energetic evolution (in your own words, of course). Let them know that you're in the process of connecting with your highest potential, which means that you're actively working to ensure that your dynamics are honest, supportive, balanced, and empowering. You may encourage them to also look within, but at the end of the day, your brave and courageous choice to self-actualize is an entirely personal decision. Accordingly, as you use these astral and physical techniques to assume a more active role in your relationships, know that the benefits transcend the bond itself. On the other side, you'll be more joyful, honest, and present in every aspect of life.

What *would* life look like if we could share our truths openly and freely? If we were safe to speak from the heart, communicating our wants, needs, and desires? Every single person is their own unique universe, which means we all have our own complex views of reality. No two people see the world through the same eyes. So, in order to maintain healthy relationships (and be an empathetic citizen of the world), we must find compassionate common ground by acknowledging our similarities and differences. Being sensitive and kind isn't just about manners—it's about being respectful of each individual's journeys.

Dismissing your truth, however, is a whole different story. If you don't prioritize your personal needs—putting others' expectations above your own, erasing your individuality to conform with your community—you are likely to wind up in unbalanced, inauthentic relationships. At the end of the day, you'll feel dissatisfied with *all* of your interpersonal dynamics, but—having forgotten who *you* are along the way—you won't be able to pinpoint what's wrong. And the longer these bonds continue, the harder it will be to connect with your truth, propelling yet another vicious cycle built on deception.

But don't worry—it doesn't need to be like this. Through a technique called **tap your truth**, you can connect with your authentic self to enhance your relationships. This exercise is for the physical realm; in other words, it requires conscious awareness in day-to-day life.

So how does it work? Whenever you're engaging with a close companion (whether it's in person, via phone, or even through text), you'll create a quiet signal to personally identify any contradictions to your truth. Whether you're experiencing this contradiction actively (for instance, saying "I'm fine" when you're actually upset) or passively (by sitting through a relative's self-obsessed forty-five-minute rant), this gentle gesture will help you realign with your core values.

You can create any signal you'd like to tap your truth, but remember that this is a private manifestation: keep the motion small and discreet. I recommend tapping your index or middle finger against your thumb a few times—this is an easy motion that you should be able to perform without raising any eyebrows. By bringing awareness to yourself, you fuse your reality with your emotions, enhancing your intuition and strengthening your conscious mind.

When you begin tapping your truth, simply performing the physical gesture may be sufficient. This small motion sends a powerful signal to the universe, confirming that—even when interpersonal relationships challenge your truth—you can always connect with your higher self. As you get more comfortable with this manifestation, however, you may want to implement changes based on the disconnect. Perhaps you'll feel empowered to adjust your interaction (for instance, you can modify your statement by saying "actually, I'm not fine, you really hurt my feelings") or even removing yourself from toxic situations (there's no reason to spend *that* much time with your egomaniacal relative).

When you hold yourself accountable to your truth, you discover that every single social interaction is a choice. This manifestation practice allows you to bring your needs to the surface, enabling you to make social decisions based on your unique realities. Remember, no two relationships are alike. No outside force can tell you what interpersonal dynamic is best suited for your individual circumstances. You, and you alone, set the standards. So when you manifest your highest potential within both the astral and physical dimensions, you form connections that reflect the full range of your consciousness. Just like the planets, your relationships mirror your reality. Enjoy your solar system!

Lovers are mirrors.

@alizakelly

FIVE

GETTING INTIMATE

"Why is it so hard for me to find love?"

"When will I meet my partner?"

"Should I reunite with my ex?"

"How can I find the right match?"

ON ROMANCE

For many, romantic compatibility is their gateway into astrology—and with good reason: celestial wisdom can offer insight for every stage of a relationship, from uncovering initial attraction to maintaining long-term commitment. Partnership is, of course, an interpersonal connection, which requires the type of consideration explored in the previous chapter. What makes romance different, however, is the *depth* of intimacy. Sex, along with other expressions of closeness (such as cohabitation, exclusivity, or marriage), create a unique type of bond that's both profoundly spiritual and terrifyingly vulnerable. Accordingly, navigating these powerful romantic connections requires special awareness. Before we begin, explore the following questions in a journal or in your mind's eye.

- When was the last time I checked in with my intimate, romantic relationships?
- In what ways has intimacy changed over time?
- In what ways has intimacy stayed the same?
- When did I last feel removed from my intimacy?
- When did I last feel connected to my intimacy?
- What helps me feel aligned with my intimacy?

ROMANCE MATTERS

This wasn't my first session with Lila. Or second. Or third. Or fourth. Truth be told, I've lost *count* of how many times I've worked with Lila. She was originally referred through a friend-of-a-friend and—as proof of how long we've known each other—she even came over to my apartment for her first birth chart reading, a practice I phased out a long time ago. The first night she visited for a session, we spent several hours exploring her birth chart, analyzing tarot spreads, and rubbing *Come to Me* oil on her phone. Don't ask.

Over the years, I watched Lila transform from a beautiful, successful woman into an *even more* beautiful, successful woman. Lila somehow balances her chic, stylish sensibilities with a super relaxed, down to earth spirit. Her energy is honest, warm, and grounded—which, I suppose, makes sense for someone with a massive Taurus stellium (Lila, born on May 12, 1983, at 4:48 A.M. in Lowell, Massachusetts, has the Sun, Moon, Rising, Mercury, Mars, and Chiron *all* occupying the sign of Taurus).

Unsurprisingly, Lila has built an incredible seven-figure business as an event planner in Manhattan. She hustles Monday through Sunday, leading champagne toasts for Fortune 500 companies, high-profile celebrities, and iconic New York City legends. It's all *very* fabulous.

From the outside, it may appear that Lila is living a tremendously perfect life and—in many ways—she is. But after a few sessions together, I found out that the glitz and glam was built around a deep-seated wound. Although her homelife was relatively uneventful, Lila was bullied relentlessly throughout school. When she was fifteen, her classmates played a horrific prank, tricking her into believing that one of the popular football jocks was interested in dating her. In a heartbreaking story that sounds like a scene from *Never Been Kissed* (1999), Lila was publicly mocked and mortified when the love letters she thought she was exchanging privately with her crush were photocopied and plastered across her high school. It was a humiliating experience that Lila never forgot and, interestingly, catalyzed her ambition.

After that trauma, Lila swore off boys and focused *exclusively* on what she could control—her academics and, subsequently, her career. Sure, she had short-lived relationships throughout college and into her early twenties, but nothing lasted for more than a few months. When I asked how those relationships ended, she simply responded, "Oh, you know. We just weren't compatible."

When Lila turned thirty-five, she realized that something needed to change. She didn't know if she wanted children, but she *definitely* wanted to be in a long-term, monogamous relationship with a reliable partner. This all sounded great, and I was thrilled when she reported that she had just started seeing someone.

"That's terrific, Lila! Tell me about him?" I asked.

"Well, he's super handsome. Really smart. Extremely hardworking. He's a little older than me—he's actually fifty-five, but that's fine because I've always preferred older men—and he's going through a pretty rough divorce, but it's okay because he's based out in Seattle so I don't have to deal with too much of the drama with the wife and the kids and the business and blah

blah blah. We text all day and, when he comes into New York we just have so much fun!"

I tried to control my expression, but—unfortunately—I don't have a very good poker face (one of the reasons that I now only work with clients via phone). She asked me why I was looking at her that way and the truth serum started flowing: "Well, Lila, this is just a little concerning. How can you build something real if he's not even in the same city? And I know love comes in all shapes and sizes, but it sounds like you might be in very different life phases? Are you *sure* he wants something serious?"

Lila assured me that everything was perfectly fine, but—several weeks later—Lila texted me with the bad news: "Mr. Seattle said he was 'too overwhelmed' to move forward. WTF?! He's such an asshole!"

"Ah, I'm sorry," I replied, "That's a shitty thing to do—but are you really surprised? I think this is for the best!"

About two weeks later, Lila called into the conference line for our monthly session. I asked how she was feeling, and was surprised by her chipper, upbeat voice. "Oh my goddddd," she gushed, "I'm so great. I can't wait to tell you about Joey!"

She met Joey just a week after Mr. Seattle disappeared into the fog of the Pacific Northwest. Joey, she explained, was thirty-six, successful, and definitely looking for something serious. But, unfortunately, he *also* didn't live in New York; Joey lived in Atlanta.

"Lila! Another long-distance guy?" I moaned.

"It's a coincidence!" She laughed—but in my practice, there are no coincidences. Clearly, there was a *reason* Lila was linking up with people who were not *actually* available for partnership. When that relationship failed (Joey wanted to give it another shot with his ex . . . who *also* lived in Atlanta), Lila continued the pattern with Antonio—a "real estate mogul"—based in England.

"Lila, who even *is* this guy? How many times have you met him?"

She'd met him during London Fashion Week and they spent ten beautiful days together. They were inseparable the entire time. He even paid to switch her flight so they could have a few more hours together before she returned to New York. "Isn't that romantic?" Lila squealed. I told her that, yeah, it could be—but if he's a real estate mogul, he's probably rich as fuck, so the cost of changing your flight was probably inconsequential. As we discussed in an earlier chapter, the value of money is different for everyone, so currency isn't always the best way to gauge interest.

"Well, when are you going to see each other again?" I asked.

Unfortunately, she sighed, she didn't know because Antonio was heading to Dubai for a few weeks, and she was going down to Austin for SXSW. But they were texting almost every day! And—honestly—Lila *always* saw herself with someone international. She and Antonio just make sense together.

Grateful this session was voice only, I closed my eyes and pressed my fingertips into my forehead. Lila's situation was dire—we needed to do some serious work . . . and fast.

✴

Astrology allows us to take a step back and understand our realities from a broader, more expansive vantage. During my one-on-one sessions, I invite clients to throw everything out on the table, so that all their truths exist in one place. I remind each client that, as a consulting astrologer, I've heard literally *everything* under the Sun; the sacred space we create together is intended for honesty, transparency, and complexity. Guided by my clients' unique circumstances, I stitch the planets' orbits into their personal realities, weaving birth chart symbolism with real-life situations.

Many, many clients come to me with questions about

romance. *Will I ever get married? When will I meet the love of my life? Who is my best match?* Of course, this isn't a surprise. Astrology and compatibility are inextricably linked (I should know; I co-founded an astrology dating app). And, like most people, my first foray into the stars was on the floor of a bookstore, pondering matters of the heart. I was about twelve years old, and I wanted to know if there was any hope for me and my crush, so I grabbed as many books and magazines as I could carry and set up shop in the corner of the Spirituality section.

Astrology verified that, as a Leo Sun, I was confident and outgoing. Generally, I have a cheery disposition, but I needed to be careful of my jealous tendencies. My crush (a Libra Sun) was *also* confident and outgoing. He loved to be in relationships but . . . uh-oh. He is extremely flirtatious and didn't want to give just one person all of his energy. *Omg*—it was *too* true!

In astrology, the Sun is an important part of your astrological profile. It symbolizes ego, essence, and sense of self. However, it's only one tiny piece of the puzzle—there are dozens upon dozens of planets, stars, and points that create a birth chart and, likewise, individual personality. At twelve, I felt like Sun sign compatibility explained absolutely everything. And that wasn't totally wrong. As you mature, you continue to grow into your chart, and it becomes increasingly clear that you cannot be defined by just your Sun sign alone—you're a whole and complete person.

What's more, when it comes to matters of the heart, you cannot limit yourself (or your partner) to a single Sun sign stereotype. After all, not all Pisces are sensitive; not all Taurus are stubborn. I'm sorry, but there's no magic cosmic compatibility formula. Astrology isn't a silver bullet, and the stars cannot simplify romance. Astrology actually *confirms* that love is often intertwined with fears, vulnerability, and doubt, making intimacy extremely messy and complex. That's why it's beautiful.

From an astrological perspective, the planet Venus plays a critical role in romance. Interestingly, despite the fact that Venus is the planet of love and beauty, the mythological origin story isn't exactly *pleasant*. According to classical antiquity, after Uranus (the primordial sky god) was castrated by his son, Cronos (better known by his Roman counterpart, Saturn), Uranus's testicles were cast into the ocean, and his severed genitalia, blood, and semen coagulated into a thick, dense foam from which Venus (or the Greek Aphrodite) was born. Delightful. (For my fellow art history nerds, this is why the canonical *Birth of Venus* painting, depicted by Sandro Botticelli and later Alexandre Cabanel, illustrates Venus rising from the sea.)

But Venus doesn't seem at all bothered by her grizzly genesis: **in the birth chart, the position of Venus governs infatuation, adoration, and romance, as well as personal taste, aesthetics, and material possessions.** Indeed your natal Venus reveals both what you want in a relationship, as well as how you approach courtship. When working with clients, I often refer to Venus as the "Marie Antoinette" of the solar system: Venus wants to nibble on decadent sweets off crystal platters, soak herself in six-hour baths, and be fanned by gigantic palm leaves.

But if Venus is so indulgent, then why is love such a shitshow? While the Venus archetype is fabulous in theory, existing in a state of constant indulgence is, of course, completely unrealistic. Though fledgling astrologers often look to Venus to gauge compatibility, this common mistake results in disappointing outcomes. You see, Venus reflects our *idealizations*, and as we explored in previous chapters, prioritizing mythologized versions of self and others is a recipe for disaster. While Venusian sensibilities are alluring, they're often constructed from fantasy as opposed to reality.

Venus's preferences can quickly devolve into superficial

intrigues and, because Venus *refuses* to remove the designer-framed rose-colored glasses, this planet struggles to differentiate "wants" from "needs." So while Venusian energy can certainly help you remodel your kitchen or host a truly epic soirée, at the end of the day, it works neither logically nor intuitively—Venus simply wants to be adored.

But Venus isn't just here to trip us up. Venus serves as a reminder that love is fabulous, and you *deserve* to be in a romantic partnership that feels totally enchanting. Likewise, noting the sign Venus occupies in your birth chart will help deepen your understanding of the most shameless expression of devotion (Table 3) and its placement via House (Table 1) as the area of life where that energy manifests. For instance, someone with Leo Venus in the Sixth House (associated with daily routines) may seek opportunities to perform—and, subsequently, attract attention—within their day-to-day environment. Alternatively, an individual who has Gemini Venus in their Eleventh House (the area of the chart that represents large-scale community) may frequently ride the line between "friend" and "lover" because they value social situations so deeply.

✖

As complicated as it may be, intimacy is an integral component of self-actualization. Lasting love happens when you're seen, appreciated, and understood by your partner, which in turn, invites you to understand yourself from a different perspective. Likewise, true partnership happens when you accept your mate as a wildly complex individual and find inspiration through both their strengths and weaknesses. You love them *because*—not in spite—of their quirks. When you find someone you're truly compatible with, you vividly illuminate each other. Each of you shine a radiant (and, *ahem*, very flattering) light on the other, resulting in an effortless exchange of exploration, optimism, and security.

And that's not to say there won't be disagreements. In fact, the best couples aren't afraid of quarreling because they know that friction fuels motion. Healthy arguments create a special kind of tension that ultimately bring couples even closer together. When you're secure in your bond, you feel comfortable in your own skin—unapologetically yourself and safe to reach your highest possible potential.

Of course, what you seek in partnership is *extremely* personal. Some, like those with a Venus in Cancer, Libra, or Capricorn, may seek more traditional partnership, while others—for instance, Venus in Aries, Sagittarius, or Aquarius—might prefer a more progressive dynamic. It should come as no surprise that Venus plays a major role in Lila's life: using a technique called *dispositors* (that is, figuring out who is the "boss" of each planet based on rulership), all of the Taurus planets and points in Lila's chart report to Venus, who is situated at 3° Cancer. Cancer is governed by the Moon, which—in Lila's chart—is located in Taurus, so the Moon and Venus are locked in a mystical union known as "mutual reception." In mutual reception, the planets are working together harmoniously, almost becoming a single unit.

Although traditional astrology would deem this flow extremely auspicious, Lila's empirical experience would say otherwise. The harmony between Lila's Venus and Moon reflects a powerful alignment between her desires and emotions, respectively. In positive circumstances, this would be a delightful celestial signature—but that wasn't Lila's reality. For Lila, Venus and the Moon were functioning as destructive enablers: The lovesick Moon was signing off on Venus's dysfunctional behavior, and Venus's insecurities were feeding the Moon's fears of inadequacy.

But you want to know something really, *really* wild? The only person who can break a cycle and recalibrate the planets to ensure a successful, happy, long-term relationship is . . . well, it's *you*. As we've already established, the physical world—including your romantic relationships—is shaped by the astral plane. In other words, your thoughts are writing the instruction manual to your reality, which means your partnerships are purely manifestations of what you, for better or worse, actually *believe* you deserve.

In a recent session, Lila asked why she keeps falling for these shitty guys (spoiler alert: Antonio turned out to be a real asshole, too). Exacerbated, I yelled, "Because you keep creating them! They're not real! They're figments of your imagination!" Yes, I know it was a trippy thing to say—but it's true. **Lovers are mirrors that reflect exactly what we want to see**. Are you always in chaotic, unreliable relationships? Do your partners consistently dip out after four weeks of dating? Is your romantic status perpetually "single"? Although it may seem like your love life is the problem, the truth is that your love life is actually just the external reaction to your internal condition. These are choices. And that is *great* news, because choices mean options, and options mean that things can change.

✖

Love has a way of really fucking with us. More than any other interpersonal dynamic, romantic relationships can send us into a tailspin. And why wouldn't they? Partnership blends vulnerability, friendship, sexuality, responsibility, finances, family. Suffice it to say, romantic partnership covers *a lot* of ground. Likewise, it's essential that we remain conscious of both *who* we connect with and, once the relationship has been established, *how* we connect with them. In other words, our process of self-reflection isn't just about meeting the right person, but also about establishing the right dynamic.

Astrology cannot simply be defined in binary "good" or "bad" terms—as we just explored with Lila's Moon-Venus mutual reception, even the most auspicious connections coincide with challenges. Using synastry charts, like the ones we calculated for Sarah and Jill in the previous chapter, we can render astrological charts to determine how each individual experiences their partner. When interpreting compatibility for a client, I look at the charts side by side (*Which House does Person A's Sun activate in Person B's chart? Which House does Person B's Moon activate in Person A's chart?*), noting both similarities and differences in the way each individual is impacted by the intimate bond.

I love the word "intimacy." It reminds me of delicate lace, like spiderwebs. Ruby-toned lighting. Fingers intertwined. Real relationships are built on intimacy. These partnerships demand transparency, honesty, and vulnerability. **In order to experience true intimacy, you need to trust your partner—but in order to trust your partner, you first need to trust yourself.** Trust that your feelings are complicated. Trust that your past is thorny. Trust that you were never, and will never be, perfect. Trust that your ability to love is limitless.

One very important component of intimacy is sex. Ah, *sex*. If only it were as simple as being horny—things would be so easy! Unfortunately, that's not reality. Sex is a complex expression of identity tangled up in a *whole* lot of psychology and spirituality and existentialism.

Have you ever wanted someone so badly, only to be horribly disappointed when you actually hook up? Or have you ever left a sexual encounter feeling drained, anxious, or insecure?

Often times, we perceive sex as the "solution" to desire, falsely believing that it will solidify someone's feelings. We believe that sex will take a relationship to the next level, or clarify whether feelings are mutual, or fuel some sort of massive emotional breakthrough.

But sex is an emotional currency, and likewise, it's essential we know what each person is exchanging. What does sex represent to you? What does sex represent to your partner? Perhaps one person desires closeness, while another desires power? One person perceives sex as an expression of commitment, while the other experiences it as mutual masturbation?

There are infinite reasons why someone would want to have sex—and yet most of the time, we just assume their reasons are the exact same as ours. This is obviously a recipe for disaster. Let's say you see sex as an act of love, but your new Tinder babe perceives sex as an exercise in dominance. Does this mean your Tinder match is . . . a bad person? Not at all! People have different relationships with sex—and that's okay. But if you don't *know* that both of you have divergent understandings of sex, you may end up feeling deeply emotionally unsatisfied.

Many astrologers differentiate the concepts of "love" and "sex" through the planets Venus and Mars, respectively. Named after the Roman god of war, it's true that Mars is all about fighting and fucking (the planet's glyph actually resembles an erect phallus and has been adopted in pop culture as the "male symbol"), but—in my experience—our sexual desire does not function in a silo. **In other words, your Mars placement (Table 3) may reveal the style with which you hump, but not necessarily *why* you're humping.** To understand the motivation behind physical urges, all of the planets and points (*What type of emotional nourishment does your Moon require? How does your natal Sun radiate? In which ways do you use Mercury to communicate your* *desires?*), along with the real-life context (that is, what's *actually* happening in your world—past and present) must be considered.

Suffice it to say, it takes time, patience, and incredible amounts of self-awareness to understand how intimacy shows up in your life. What's more, it's not always easy to acknowledge, especially because your default relationship style is the physical embodiment of your greatest fears. Yes, you read that correctly. It may seem counterproductive, but it's actually pretty straightforward: **we want what we fear we lack.** If this reminds you of wisdoms surrounding money, you're absolutely correct. Scarcity thinking doesn't just apply to resources—it extends to our romantic relationships, as well.

In the same way that desperation blocks financial abundance, desperation also obstructs healthy romance. Whatever you're cooking in your astral kitchen will be served, piping hot, in the physical domain. For many of us, that anxiety ends up manifesting in our real-life relationships. But fear doesn't exercise good judgment. In fact, relationships built on deep-seated insecurities end up fueling vicious cycles.

My client, Renee, is a great example. Renee was obsessed with marrying someone rich. So when she met her boyfriend—a cutthroat investment banker with "high earning potential"—she was certain she'd found the perfect man. Renee's fixation on wealth wasn't because she was intrinsically superficial or materialistic; it was because, in her childhood, money symbolized love. So, in her attempt to find someone wealthy, she mistakenly believed she would guarantee long-term commitment and emotional intimacy, as well. But while love is stable and enduring, money is volatile. Likewise, the relationship was deeply disenchanting for Renee—no matter what her boyfriend did or didn't do, she never felt like it was enough. The issue, of course, is that she didn't enter that relationship because she loved *him* as a person; she entered the relationship because she loved what he *represented*. And these are totally different things.

Another client, Avery, also encountered this in her relationships. Like so many of us, Avery struggles with self-esteem, and—over the years—created a false narrative that all "good matches" were "out of her league." So Avery settled for someone she thought would be a "safe bet"—someone she thought would be *thrilled* to be Avery's girlfriend and accordingly, would never run off with a cooler, prettier girl.

In reality, however, Avery's "safe" girlfriend was someone who *also* struggled with confidence: she was unmotivated, unhappy, and extremely codependent. But, because Avery entered the relationship out of desperation (scarcity thinking at its finest), she wasn't actually considering who her girlfriend was, but rather, who she *assumed* she was. Ironically, her girlfriend wasn't just unsafe, but actually incredibly toxic. She was rude, bitter, and unfaithful. Avery was betrayed yet again—only this time, by someone she didn't even want in the first place.

The moral? **When you let fear pick your partner, you end up dating the physical embodiment of your anxieties.** Yikes.

But, hey. We're all human. We make mistakes—and that's totally fine. The bigger issue, however, is when we don't take accountability for our choices. Indeed, denial is intimacy's mortal enemy—it's the very reason Lila's love life is such a debacle. Despite the fact that Lila's behavior is quite *obviously* repetitive, she refuses to acknowledge the pattern. Further, the reason she refuses to acknowledge the pattern is because she's afraid to admit what she really wants.

If you can't be honest with yourself in the astral realm, you cannot build an honest romantic relationship in the

physical realm. Remember, we're constantly in the process of manifesting our realities—we are incredibly powerful cosmic beings. So, if you're lying to *yourself* about what you want, it's energetically impossible for you to connect with the right partner.

For Lila, justifying these unrewarding partnerships was an attempt to convince herself that these unavailable men actually offered what she wanted. That this was the best she could get. Despite the fact that these long-distance texters were imitation boyfriends, she was inadvertently preventing herself from meeting the right person—and, in a way, that's what she wanted. Because meeting an available partner would actually *require* her to be vulnerable, and Lila wasn't prepared to do that.

Sadly, Lila believed that—as an "imperfect" person—*no one* would *actually* be interested in building something real with her. So, rather than risk rejection, Lila connected with people who were *quite clearly* incapable of cultivating an authentic, lasting relationship. And, although this behavior may seem counterproductive, it *is* successfully reinforcing Lila's self-deprecating narrative: all of these failed "partnerships" *prove* Lila's hypothesis, validating her alleged romantic ineptitude.

"Lila, you knew you were never going to have a real relationship with Antonio. And, to be honest, he knew that you weren't looking for one, either." I said in a recent session.

"What do you mean?" she asked.

"Because, if you were looking for a serious relationship, you wouldn't have dated him."

✳

If you want to meet the right person, you need to be available. I know, I know—easier said than done. Maybe you're addicted to the chase. After all, dating apps are built around quick hits of validation—and, no matter how complimentary your partner may be, no serious relationship has the ability to compete with the instant gratification of likes and swipes and matches.

Or maybe you get stuck in the fantasy—the illusion of what *could* have been. You want so *badly* for it to work. Consumed by the idea of the relationship that exists solely in your imagination, you desperately try to will it into reality. But that's not how manifestation works: we cannot control other people. So, if you're spending all your energetic power trying to build a relationship with someone who's simply unavailable, the results are going to be . . . messy. And this can go on and on, but the longer it continues, the longer it takes for you to meet the person who can *actually* show up in a meaningful way.

Since you are solely responsible for honoring your truth, intimacy (including sex) requires complete and total transparency: there is absolutely no room for denial. **In order to create real, long-lasting romantic bonds, you must practice fearless self-awareness in both the etheric and physical realms.**

For many of us, intimacy is one of the hardest things to crack. And why shouldn't it be—intimacy is the *definition* of vulnerability. But as you pull back the curtain and explore the nooks and crannies of every aspect of your life, empowering yourself to truly embody your destiny, it becomes increasingly obvious that romantic partnership is an extension of your consciousness. Likewise, these relationships require careful analysis and hard work. We cannot fully self-actualize *until* we truly understand what intimacy means to us individually.

Of course, this is not a one-size-fits-all. While some people seek traditional commitment and marriage, others will prefer more open, flexible dynamics. Some people may not want to have a partnership at all and choose to maintain their autonomy as a single individual. All of these are absolutely fine. There is no hierarchy, one approach isn't better than the other. Celebrate whatever makes sense for you—it's personal.

What should be noted, however, is that **your approach to partnership is a choice, not an obligation.** The way you connect (or don't connect) with others has major implications because it's a direct line into your psyche. Through awareness, you solidify your understanding of self by opening a portal into your potential. Ultimately, choosing *not* to partner is the same as choosing *to* partner. Either way, you're making a decision about the way you relate to others, and correspondingly, the way others relate to you. This is very different from passive acceptance. Throwing your hands up and agreeing to something because it's easy or available or because you think you won't get any better is *not*—in any world whatsoever—a choice; it's forfeiting.

Saying "yes" to something you don't want—whether it's a person or relationship dynamic—sends an indisputable message to the universe that you're *not* manifesting your best life. That you are *not* interested in honoring your truth and reaching your highest potential. That you do *not* listen to your intuition. Slowly but surely, this doubt trickles into every aspect of your reality, obstructing the cycle of manifestation and preventing you from self-actualization. Yes, it's extreme . . . but unfortunately, I'm not exaggerating.

At the end of the day, every partnership (including the absence of partnership) requires active awareness. Are you unhappy with your current romantic situation? No problem!

The below manifestations will help you get back on track. Already in a happy, long-term relationship? Great! It's essential that you *continue* infusing your romantic bond through mindfulness—after all, we're taking charge of our intimacy, and maintenance is essential. Without upkeep, even the most exquisite structures can go into disrepair.

ROMANCE REVIEW

- Intimate relationships are complex dynamics that are linked to many facets of consciousness
- Fear, denial, and/or insecurities prevent us from cultivating honest, vulnerable, sustainable dynamics
- Toxic cycles can be broken through active self-awareness
- Venus reveals how we want to be adored; Mars symbolizes our motivation (including sexual urges)

MANIFESTATIONS FOR ROMANCE

Internal (Astral): Send It Love

As we explored throughout this chapter, the biggest obstacle in finding (and keeping) lasting love is self-doubt. When we approach our romantic relationships through fear, we end up connecting with people who are—in cruel irony—the living embodiment of that anxiety. I'm sorry to say desperation is *not* a good matchmaker; nervous energy doesn't have your best interests in mind.

Suffice it to say, you connect with people who are tangible extensions of your psyche. But don't worry, the astral plane is an adaptable landscape shaped by your compassionate consciousness. This internal, reflective exercise is called **Send It Love** and it's quite straightforward.

Grab a piece of a paper or clean page in your journal and list three of your biggest self-criticisms. No more, no less. This exercise isn't about assembling a laundry list of weaknesses—it's about bringing focused attention to your perceived "flaws," so you can identify which negative thoughts are most actively influencing your psyche. You can pull from any dimension that makes sense to you: these "flaws" can be personality traits, past experiences, physical characteristics, or emotional attributes. If you cannot compile a list of three self-criticisms, let that also guide this exercise: Have you self-actualized so much that you are *truly* at peace with every part of yourself, or (*ahem*) are you refusing to be vulnerable even with *yourself*?

Once you've created your list, we move on to phase two—this is where it gets good. Ultimately, we're going to repurpose these traits by upgrading them from self-doubts to psychic-warriors. These attributes are going to become spiritual vigilantes that have the executive power to convert any other self-perceived weaknesses into fully-realized strengths. Believe it or not, these three attributes are about to become your etheric cheerleaders. But before we release them back into the wild, we need to send 'em some love.

In order for these traits to confidently step into their new roles, you need to make sure they're empowered. Next to each attribute, write down some of its innate gifts. How can you shift your perception to ensure that it's working *for* you, not against you?

For instance, if you identified "perfectionism" as a negative attribute, explore its positive components—maybe you're organized, detail-oriented, and reliable? Maybe you're great at coming up with systems, and you can help your more scattered friends when they're drowning in chaos? If you listed something physical, say "your stomach," imagine this feature from a different lens. Maybe your stomach is soft and round—a classic symbol of divine femininity? Maybe you store your feelings in this body part? Maybe this area is the epicenter of your intuition?

This exercise may not be easy; after all, you've likely spent many, many years seeking vengeance on these very attributes. But you're the one writing your story, and now you're incorporating a plot twist into the narrative. You're not just finding compassion for these traits—you're actually giving them *value.* Likewise, these qualities are now on your team, and motivated by love, they'll be sure to help you quell any future self-doubt *coups d'état.*

There's no reason to sabotage yourself by willing your fears into existence. Your reality is an extension of the psychic dimension, and likewise, you want to transform the astral realm into an inspiring, supportive landscape that embraces your full and complete self. You're welcome to perform this manifestation whenever you desire an energetic shift—whether you're going on a first date or simply looking to go deeper with your existing bond. After all, if love really is a battlefield, you want to make sure you're fired up and ready to go.

Attributes . . . assemble!

External (Physical): Change Something

If you're unhappy with your reality, should you:

A. Do nothing
B. Change something

The answer is, of course, *(B) Change something.* And I'm sure you passed with flying colors because, to be quite honest, *(A) Do nothing* looks pretty silly contextualized in this format. But as we move through life, we don't always have multiple choice questions that neatly lay out our options, making it easy for us to select the better choice. And, even if we did, implementing them is still an entirely different story.

We don't often address problems proactively. Most of the time, even after an issue has been identified, we don't do anything about it. This may be because we don't want to leave our comfort zone, or because we don't know how to approach the situation from a different angle. Either way, we often find ourselves uninspired, unsatisfied, and deeply disappointed by our circumstances.

This happens quite frequently in romantic relationships. Whether you're not meeting the right lovers, are constantly bickering with your partner, or have found yourself trapped in a humdrum malaise, you're not getting what you desire. But yet, you continue doing the same thing—maybe you're hoping that, next time, things will be different? Maybe you're scared of creating *more* problems? Maybe, at some point down the line, you even wrote off joy, accepting that you were never going to get exactly what you want?

Forfeiting ends right here, right now. You are in the process of self-actualizing, which means you're empowered to make thoughtful, active choices that celebrate your highest purpose. And when it comes to love, if you're not happy with the way something is going . . . well, it's time to do something about it!

This external manifestation (that is, to be performed

actively within the physical realm) is called **change something** and, well, it's pretty literal. If you keep dating people who end up disappearing after six weeks, it's time to change something. Or, if you haven't connected with someone in five months because you're still pining for your ex, it's time to change something. If you want to reach a deeper level of emotional connection with your partner, it's time to change something.

By challenging your personal status quo and choosing to take action, you create the space to breathe new life into any situation. This is a wonderfully productive manifestation because it, quite literally, activates your destiny. Your reality is a construction of your consciousness, which means you're *not* at the mercy of external obstacles. You don't need to wait for your partner to make the first move. Happiness falls within your purview, so you have the ability to construct a romantic life that reflects your truth.

But, again, I know that change can be easier said than done. After all, your scope is limited to your perspective; maybe you don't have any ideas? No problem; I've compiled a list of fifty ways you can change something. You may find a change that perfectly captures the spirit of your situation, or you may need to make slight adjustments to apply it to your unique circumstances. Ultimately, this list should serve as a dynamic meditation—an active reminder that, when it comes to self-actualization, even a slight shift can catalyze a tremendous transformation.

So, whenever you need to improve something in your romantic life, be sure to perform this manifestation. At the end of the day, the worst thing that could happen is that things remain the same. Go ahead—change something!

1. You aren't making any romantic connections, so create a profile on a dating app.
2. You aren't making any romantic connections, so deactivate your dating profile.
3. You aren't making any romantic connections, so ask your friends for help.
4. You aren't making any romantic connections, so reevaluate what you're looking for.
5. You aren't making any romantic connections, so stop texting your ex.
6. Your relationships end prematurely, so don't enter relationships too early.
7. Your relationships end prematurely, so ask what your significant other is looking for.
8. Your relationships end prematurely, so lead with your truth.
9. Your relationships end prematurely, so protect your emotions.
10. Your relationships end prematurely, so connect with the right people.
11. You feel insecure, so discuss your fears with your significant other.
12. You feel insecure, so explore your fears on your own.
13. You feel insecure, so ask your partner to adjust their behavior.
14. You feel insecure, so trust your intuition.
15. You feel insecure, so avoid self-sabotage.
16. You want your partner to make a commitment, so make a commitment to your partner.
17. You want your partner to make a commitment, so don't text them as often.

18. You want your partner to make a commitment, so be straightforward.
19. You want your partner to make a commitment, so have fun.
20. You want your partner to make a commitment, so demand that you're taken seriously.
21. The sex isn't working, so stop having sex.
22. The sex isn't working, so have more sex.
23. The sex isn't working, so talk about sex.
24. The sex isn't working, so stop talking about sex.
25. The sex isn't working, so seek expert advice.
26. You're worried they're cheating, so confront them.
27. You're worried they're cheating, so give them more space.
28. You're worried they're cheating, so give them less space.
29. You're worried they're cheating, so define your expectations.
30. You're worried they're cheating, so end the relationship.
31. You're not getting along, so address the tension.
32. You're not getting along, so don't jump to conclusions.
33. You're not getting along, so spend more time together.
34. You're not getting along, so spend more time apart.
35. You're not getting along, so let go of the problem.
36. You want to break up, so break up.
37. You want to break up, so discuss the problem.
38. You want to break up, so spend time apart.
39. You want to break up, so spend time together.
40. You want to break up, so seek expert advice.
41. You're bored, so take a vacation together.
42. You're bored, so take a vacation apart.
43. You're bored, so have more sex.
44. You're bored, so have less sex.
45. You're bored, so adopt a plant.

46. You want the relationship to last, so make a commitment.
47. You want the relationship to last, so find independence.
48. You want the relationship to last, so be brutally honest.
49. You want the relationship to last, so listen more.
50. You want the relationship to last, so don't go anywhere.

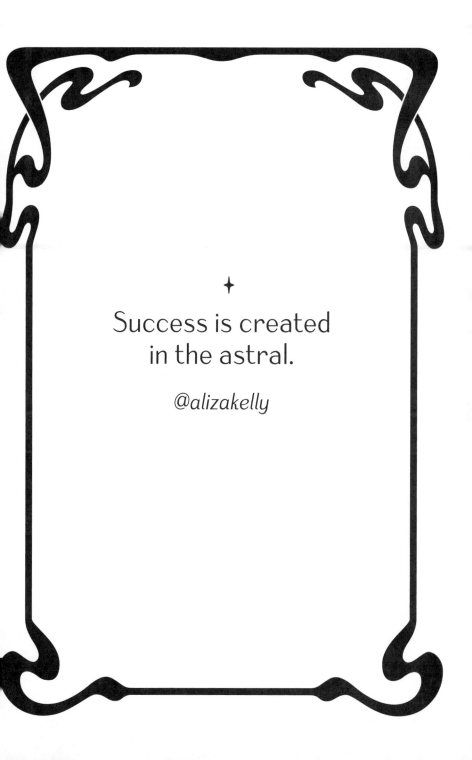

✦

Success is created
in the astral.

@alizakelly

SIX

HUSTLE WITH INTENTION

"Am I on the right track?"

"Should I quit my job?"

"Will I ever be able to accomplish my goals?"

"What will it take to achieve success?"

ON CAREER

Before diving into this chapter, let's clarify a very important truth: career is not synonymous with purpose. Your career is the through-line of your professional pursuits; your purpose, on the other hand, transcends vocation. For some, career and purpose might overlap, but—like all topics addressed in this book—the way these concepts do or don't coexist should be adjusted to fit your circumstances. Suffice it to say, we spend the vast majority of our adult lives working, so cultivating an enjoyable career, *regardless* of whether it aligns with your individual definition of purpose, is meaningful. In fact, some of the most frequently asked questions in my one-on-one client sessions relate to professional pursuits. So, whether you're interested in turning your part-time hobby into a full-time job, finding a deeper appreciation for your current employment, or letting the stars guide your path, exploring your career through an astrological vantage will offer invaluable perspective. First, here are a few questions to consider in a journal or your mind's eye.

- When was the last time I checked in with my career?
- In what ways have my professional passions changed over time?
- In what ways have my professional passions stayed the same?
- When did I last feel successful?
- When did I last feel unsuccessful?
- What helps me align with my career?

CAREER MATTERS

Some astrologers prepare birth charts hours—even days—ahead of their sessions. Before they connect with their clients, they'll meticulously analyze the planets and Houses and aspects, identifying key dates and overarching themes. Then, when the birth chart reading begins, the astrologer may ask a number of clarifying questions to guide the session in the direction of the cosmos.

This is a terrific approach. But it's not mine.

Well, that's not completely true. When I first began my practice, I would spend quite some time studying the birth chart before I spoke with the client. Really, I wanted to make sure that I could fill the sixty-minute session with insight and observations. I dreaded even a moment of silence—I was determined to offer the most dynamic, mystical, thought-provoking experience imaginable.

But, as I expanded my practice, it became increasingly evident that "running out" of astrological interpretations was not the problem. Quite the opposite, my one-hour sessions would go way over time, lasting two, three, even four hours. This obviously impacted my personal life, and I became more and more unreliable—I couldn't keep plans with my friends or family because, when I had an astrology session, I had no way of knowing how long it would last. What if something I say strikes a chord? What if they want to go deeper? What if they have more questions?

Through experience, I learned that time boundaries weren't just a function of my daily schedule, they actually *improved* the experience for the client, as well. Like astrology, a single birth chart is infinite—but that doesn't mean a birth chart session needs to be. I began to realize that I didn't need to share every single observation I could muster, but rather, carefully interpret the specific topics the client wanted to explore. There's always a reason someone is interested in working with an astrologer and, by leading with the topics and issues they're interested in exploring (as opposed to my free-association observations sans context), we use time as a tool to aid the extraction process.

But when Bianca's birth chart appeared on my screen, I had a hunch that I knew what Bianca would want to discuss. Born on January 29, 1989 at 2:42 P.M. in Fort Lauderdale, Florida, Bianca was twenty-nine, which meant she was in the midst of her first Saturn Return—an important astrological milestone that distinguishes your future from your past. **It's during our Saturn Return that we grow up, define our identity, and carve out our place in the world.** Often, the years right before your Saturn Return are jam-packed with unprecedented, life-changing events.

Although the Saturn Return looks different for everyone, we know it always coincidences with extraordinary transformation.

As soon as I met Bianca on the astral plane (a.k.a. the conference line), it was clear that Saturn was already in full swing. At the beginning of our session, Bianca told me about how she had spent the past several years working at a healthcare technology company. She loved the company, her colleagues, and she even loved her boss. And then one day, she woke up and realized she didn't want to do it anymore. So she put in her two weeks' notice and called it quits.

"It was totally unexpected," she explained. "But it was like something shifted within me and I just had this sense of urgency like if I didn't leave right then, I would never get out. And I'm so scared I made a mistake."

I told her that I understood; that definitely sounded like a bold move. And I also told her that this was the exact right time in her life to challenge herself and step outside the comfort zone. Saturn Return marks a critical moment of self-discovery— there's no better time to shake up your status quo than when Saturn comes around.

Saturn Return refers to Saturn's orbit: approximately every twenty-nine years, Saturn completes a cycle and "returns" to the position it occupied when you were born (see Table 2). You can actually have three Saturn Returns in your lifetime: the first in your late twenties, the second in your late fifties, and the third in your late eighties.

Suffice it to say, Saturn has a bit of a *reputation*. Historically, Saturn has been associated with death, misery, and even the Devil himself. Much of Saturn's mythology was adopted from the Greek story of Cronus. Uranus and Gaia birthed several children—the Titans—one of whom was Cronus, or Saturn. Uranus became increasingly paranoid that his children would overthrow him, so one by one, he cast them into the depths of the Earth. Gaia was not pleased with Uranus's hostility, and presented her son Cronus-Saturn with a scythe to attack Uranus, putting a stop to his delusional antics. (Fun fact: Did you know the Grim Reaper is based on Saturn and his scythe?) With this tool, Saturn castrated his father. Uranus's testicles dropped into the ocean (ultimately becoming Venus), and Uranus was banished into the depths of the sky.

But trauma runs through bloodlines, and—once Saturn became a father—he ended up repeating the same exact behavior. After Uranus was exiled, Saturn assumed the title King of the Gods. Saturn had several children with Opis, but just like his father, became increasingly anxious and tyrannical. As an attempt to maintain the throne, he began consuming his infant children. (Art history lovers may recall the canonical work *Saturn Devouring His Son* as depicted by Peter Paul Rubens and, later, Francisco Goya). Just as Gaia aided Saturn's coup, Opis managed to save her son, Zeus-Jupiter, by hiding him in a cave, feeding Saturn a bag of rocks instead of the child (clearly, Saturn didn't have a very sophisticated palette). Eventually, Jupiter grew strong enough to overthrow Saturn, forcing him to regurgitate his digested siblings (Neptune, Pluto, Juno, Ceres, and Vesta).

Saturn was then banished to Italy, where he established himself in Latium (the capital city of the Roman Empire). Under his rule, the metropolis prospered as an agricultural center (all thanks to Saturn's scythe!). Legend has it that the Latium people, who were known for their hedonistic behavior, were soothed by Saturn's stern and sober approach, and eventually adopted an orderly lifestyle—a true success story.

Saturn's story appears in astrology, as well: this ringed-gas giant represents tradition, wisdom, and maturity, as well as life's most difficult challenges. Have you ever heard of the "seven-year itch?" From an astrological point of view, that's part of Saturn's cycle. Every seven years—one quarter of a Saturn orbit—Saturn squares prompt cataclysmic change, so whether you're leaving a marriage, quitting your job, or recalibrating your life's purpose, Saturn is demanding you take full and complete responsibility as you commit to personal growth in seven-year intervals.

The Saturn cycle concludes with the Saturn Return, which occurs for the first time in your late twenties. During the Saturn Return, we are often moved to reevaluate our place in the world, separating our purpose from the template set forth by our external influences (such as parents, teachers, peers, and greater society). On the other side of Saturn Return, we reemerge as our own "fathers," so to speak. We report to ourselves—we make our own rules. We give less shits about what others think about us. Likewise, our professional trajectory is often aligned with Saturn.

But career can't be attributed to Saturn alone. Another astrological device used to indicate career is a point on your birth chart called the Midheaven (or Medium Coeli, Latin for "middle of the sky"). **When looking at your birth chart, the Midheaven appears at the very top of the wheel (at the twelve o'clock position), and likewise, indicates the "peak" of your professional achievements.** Astrologers read the birth chart like a clock. We enter the chart at the Ascendant (which is located at the nine o'clock position) and move—counterclockwise—across the entire face of the wheel. From this vantage, we need to traverse 75 percent of our birth chart *before* we reach the Midheaven point. **In other words, we cannot access our highest professional potential until we've amassed enough life experience (and, honestly, momentum) to hurl ourselves up the mountain.** This is an important reminder that it takes *years and years* to cultivate your career. Although greater society idolizes youth culture (superlatives such as *Forbes* 30 Under 30 imply that success achieved by thirty is the best kind of success), this *does not* mirror our organic, cosmic timing. Professional achievement is a lifelong process.

There's another astrological wisdom that offers insight on career. The tenth zodiac sign, Capricorn, is represented by the majestic sea-goat—a mythological creature that has the body of a goat and the tail of a fish. Capricorn's bifurcated anatomy illustrates how this sign can effortlessly scale mountains (representing success on the physical plane), as well as navigate unseen, subterranean landscapes (revealing their mastery within the etheric realm). Sound familiar? Of course, there are no coincidences: Capricorn's twofold approach to manifestation (internal and external) mirrors the self-actualization practices outlined in this book and (naturally) within the universe.

Because each person has every zodiac sign embedded in their birth chart, Capricorn energy is nestled within you, too. Regardless of whether you have any planets in Capricorn, you can tap into this powerful, professionally-motivated energy whenever you desire. Certainly, the transiting planets (that is, the planets moving in real time) will also impact when and how you experience these Capricorn sensibilities, but ultimately, you can start or end cycles at will. Never ignore your desire to take action.

It's important to remember that your career is not the same thing as finances (for a refresher on money matters, head back to chapter 3). There is, of course, a powerful connection between career and capital—likewise, many people will experience obstructions in both of these domains simultaneously. However, the obstacles we may encounter relating to career and money, respectively, are quite distinctive, so it's important to "treat" them independently.

We can see this exemplified through my time working

one-on-one with Derek. When Derek and I started our session, he told me he was having "career problems." Upon conversation, it became clear that Derek was stuck in a fear-based *financial* feedback loop. He constantly felt like his back was against the wall, and thus kept accepting odd jobs to pay his bills. Despite working fifty- and sixty-hour weeks, however, Derek couldn't seem to dig himself out of this financial hole. "Derek, once you generate financial abundance, do you feel like you're going to be successful?" His response was an enthusiastic, "Hell yes!" Identifying this as a money issue as opposed to a career issue, I encouraged Derek to use the manifestation techniques outlined in chapter 3 (both the internal and external).

Money lack says "I'll never *have* enough," whereas professional lack says "I'll never *be* enough." Career blockages aren't the byproduct of external circumstances, but rather, stem from a deeply rooted belief that there is a limit to your individual success. There are endless reasons that someone may develop this mindset (unsupportive parents, societal expectations, childhood disappointments . . .) and, of course, context provides deep insight into an individual's unique journey. But regardless of what sparked this feedback loop, we know that—because we're always manifesting the truth of our psyche—we'll continue to reinforce that narrative until we *actively* choose to break the cycle.

When we remove financial anxieties from the equation, it's much easier to identify professional lack. Naomi, my long-term client, is from an extremely wealthy family. She was raised in Beverly Hills and, through various trusts set up by her parents and grandparents, has more and more access to financial resources as she continues to get older.

Despite the fact that Naomi is extremely financially privileged, however, she continues to suffer from professional lack. Naomi wants to be a successful singer-songwriter, but is constantly sabotaging herself through self-doubt. Naomi is afraid no one will take her seriously because of her family's affluence. "Real rock stars need to struggle," she once said.

I countered, "What about the Strokes? Or Carly Simon? Or Nancy Sinatra? There are tons of well-respected artists who come from privilege."

"I don't know . . ." she continued, "why should I think I'm so special?"

"The issue is that you don't think you're special *enough*."

Though Naomi inherited financial abundance, her professional insecurities were causing her serious psychic suffering. The boundaries she placed on her success in the astral realm prevent her from collaborating, releasing songs, and even performing live. Sure, Naomi may have the ability to invest in her career—but deep-seated scarcity mentality is blocking her from actualizing her full potential.

At this point, the skeptical reader may wonder if we're conflating scarcity mentality with realistic expectations. After all, not *every* artist can become successful at their craft, right? When does following a dream become chasing a delusion?

And yes, excellent point. In order to advance professionally, we need external opportunities and—since everyone is drifting through their own journeys—things don't always move as quickly as we'd hope. It's true that there are infinite obstacles in our day-to-day realities. There are so many things that could go wrong that would prevent us from reaching our highest potential. But that's why it's absolutely *essential* the astral dimension remains free-flowing and unencumbered.

There are countless roadblocks in the physical realm, yet, some people manage to sidestep hurdles and overcome impossible odds. **Success demands psychic fortitude.** Simply put, you'll never be able to turn your dreams into reality if you don't give yourself permission to believe it's possible.

Further, the significance of your career is based on your unique circumstances. For instance, if you had parents who were obsessed with their professional reputation, you may not want to pursue a high-pressure path. Perhaps you would rather explore a vocation that offers you the time and space to explore passion projects or give back to your community through full-time activism. Alternatively, you may be someone who deeply desires fame and fortune—there's nothing wrong with that! But in order for you to self-actualize, you will need to commit to your calling. When it comes to living your best life, there's no time to cut corners.

To clarify terminology, it's important that we distinguish "job" from "career." Jobs are directly linked to our day-to-day realities. Jobs play a huge role in our life, because they reveal how we exchange our time for money. Your career will be *realized* through jobs, but jobs are not your career. Your jobs don't need to have a "bigger purpose"—sometimes, we just need to pay our bills. Career is something totally separate.

I often remind younger clients that it's *good* to feel restless and uncertain in your twenties. According to astrology, the process of professional actualization doesn't even *begin* until your first Saturn Return. And Saturn governs with a "tough love" approach, which means this stern taskmaster is guaranteed to challenge your preconceived notions of success one way or another—so any professional path explored in your twenties will likely go through a massive overhaul by the time you reach your early thirties.

This was certainly true in Bianca's case. Although she still couldn't pinpoint exactly what compelled her to leave, she knew she needed to break her routine. What I appreciate about Bianca's story is that she *didn't* have a backup plan. She didn't have another job offer waiting in the wings. She wasn't sitting on a passion project. There wasn't another industry she wanted to explore. **The big risk was, in fact, the risk itself.**

We live in a world of instant gratification. We want our movies now, our packages tomorrow, and overnight success . . . like, yesterday. And while there are many advantages to our modern, automated world, not *everything* can—or should—be expedited.

Careers take time to build; your professional peak is an amalgamation of all your experience, including your successes and failures. Indeed, the journey to professional actualization is not linear. Sometimes, you'll need to move laterally until you find a new path forward. Every now and then, it may even seem like you're backpedaling. While this may be frustrating in the moment, it's essential to remember that the sum of the whole is always greater than its parts. Even when you can't quite see the peak, trust that you're in the process of scaling something monumental—something that can only be revealed through time and vantage.

However, just because your professional achievements exist on a macro level doesn't mean that you shouldn't fine-tune in the microsphere. Perhaps you don't yet know what type of career to explore? Or maybe you want confirmation that you're on the right path? If you've already honed in on your perfect upward trajectory, you might be wondering how you can take your day-to-day to the next level?

Your destiny isn't your career—but your career *is* part of your destiny. So what does that mean? You're guiding your journey, so you can actively shape your professional future every step of the way. Likewise, these two manifestations (one for the internal astral plane, and the other for the external physical world) will not only help you reach your goals, but also enable you to achieve exceptional results. Remember, in order to live an extraordinary life, you must dream beyond boundaries. In the words of Cady Heron from *Mean Girls* (2004), "the limit does not exist!"

CAREER REVIEW

- Career is neither your purpose, nor is it your job; career is the amalgamation of your professional pursuits cultivated over a lifetime
- Bravery is an integral component of success
- Give yourself permission to dream big
- Saturn, the Midheaven, and the sign of Capricorn offer meaningful insight about professional pursuits

MANIFESTATIONS FOR CAREER

Internal (Astral): Words to Live By

Success can be intimidating! First, you need to find the right opportunities, which are few and far between. But then there's so much competition! How do you stand out from the noise? No matter what industry you're in, there are countless other qualified candidates who surely excel in the exact skill you're lacking. So, among all of the variables, wouldn't your chances of "making it" be, like, one in a million?

Yes. Your self-doubt will be thrilled to know that I am fully and completely aware of how difficult it is to reach your highest professional potential. Trust me, I really get it. I'm an astrologer.

But now that we've acknowledged probability, you never need to think about it again. Because, to be perfectly honest, there's no point. Sure, there are endless reasons why things *wouldn't* work out—but, for better or worse, those variables are entirely out of your control.

From now on, whenever you find yourself pulled toward cynicism, let your doubts slingshot you forward. All of the external forces that would limit your success are *not* your responsibility. In fact, *every* success story could be deemed impossible, because **careers are built in the astral.** Likewise, when it comes to your professional goals, your internal reality needs to be *so* confident, *so* optimistic, *so* shameless that it triumphs over the inevitable roadblocks.

To cultivate professional abundance, your vantage should extend *beyond* your mind's eye—symbolizing the boundless, unprecedented opportunities that await. Invite your doubts to melt away; they're no longer needed within this psyche. From here on out, your subconscious green-lights your success.

Now that you're all set up, you're ready to align with your professional purpose and find the **words to live by**. From the list on page 155, select whichever words you would like infused within your career. Don't worry about your current job or employment prospects; your choices shouldn't mimic the assumed descriptors for a particular occupation, but rather, reveal your broad range of desires. As with all of our manifestations, your honest assessment is of the utmost importance—this exercise is for your own self-improvement, so don't bungle your answers with inauthentic selections. Your truth is the fastest route to empowerment.

Once you've completed this exercise, ruminate on the words. Which are reflected in your professional reality today? Which are not? Do the words fit together harmoniously, or are there contradictions? Are you currently embodying these terms, or are you resisting their presence?

Next, consider ways you can continue to instill these terms within your psyche. You may want to write them on sticky notes that you place in a highly trafficked area of your home or office (like on the edge of a mirror or around your computer screen), "set them" as alarms throughout the day, or create phrases to embed them in your consciousness (for instance, "I Am The Boss" would be a great mnemonic for the words Intellectual, Adventurous, Thrilling, Bold).

When you find your words to live by, you'll be sure that—no matter what jobs you take along the way—you're cultivating a professional legacy that aligns with your desires. Don't forget, you're building a career in your image . . . not the other way around!

Quality	Fair	Courageous
Leadership	Cheerful	Cultured
Reputation	Helpful	Curious
Corporate	Industrious	Daring
Structured	Healing	Dependable
Wealth	Honest	Diplomatic
Celebrity	Assertive	Easygoing
Status	Attentive	Efficient
Access	Committed	Energetic
Generosity	Dynamic	Entrepreneurial
Philanthropy	Imaginative	Ethical
Functional	Artistic	Ease
Iconic	Ambitious	Relaxation
Distinguished	Analytical	Choice
Prolific	Authentic	Recognition
Intellectual	Balanced	Acceptance
Thrilling	Brave	Progressive
Bold	Wild	Political
Adventurous	Safe	Social
Inventive	Security	Tender
Exciting	Guidance	Supportive
Thoughtful	Teaching	Busy
Powerful	Learning	Trailblazing
Practical	Cutthroat	Unprecedented
Original	Spotlight	Fancy
Active	Attention	Fast
Positive	Privacy	Flexible
Consistent	Intimacy	Passionate
Compassionate	Partnership	Strategic
Incredible	Relaxed	Competitive
Independent	Inspired	Technological
Precise	Humanitarianism	Collaborative

External (Physical): One Step at a Time

So now that we *no longer speak of professional roadblocks* (Right? Right!), we can start incorporating our manifestation into the physical domain, as well. By working within both the internal and external dimensions, you create a feedback loop that offers comprehensive support through your self-actualization process. The more you exercise both of these techniques, the stronger this link becomes. Ultimately, investing in both of these practices will enable you to build such an airtight system that it is impervious to obstruction.

So what are you waiting for? All you need to do is take **one step at a time.** The technique is extremely simple (but shockingly effective). In order to manifest your career in the physical world, do one proactive thing for your career each and every day.

Yes, that's it—one simple thing. The only parameter is that these gestures need to be action-oriented within the physical world, so they must be external as opposed to reflective. For instance, writing a to-do list, brainstorming a five-year plan, or daydreaming about your future corner office *would not* count. Don't get me wrong—these are all terrific things that could surely elevate your success, but they're not outward movements. On the other hand, sending a cold email, arranging new headshots, or attending a networking event are all excellent options for this exercise. They need to be proactive; not reflective.

This manifestation is not theoretical, it could not exist *without* the external realm. Likewise, this manifestation bonds your intention with your reality, enabling you to take an active role in your career. Since long-term success will undoubtedly require some level of participation from outside sources (customers, bosses, clients, followers, etc.), fortifying your own daily practice will enable you to assume even more agency in this aspect of your life.

Another thing to note is that this manifestation works quickly—like, *really* quickly. In fact, as you begin this exercise, you may realize that your career is moving faster than you anticipated. I used this technique when I was first building my private astrology practice, and within about six weeks, my schedule was totally at capacity. Likewise, even if you're feeling super ambitious, I would not exceed the daily limit. Believe it or not, there is too much of a good thing, and if you generate excess abundance before you're ready, you may end up inadvertently burning a few bridges (or burning out). This is like the professional equivalent of stepping into a financial surplus before you've turned up your thermostat (as discussed in chapter 3); in short, you could end up with more work than you want.

If you prefer a slower incline or your calendar is *already* pushed to the limit, you can reduce the frequency of this manifestation, practicing the technique two or three times per week instead of daily. After all, this isn't just about competing tasks; it's about fortifying new connections to the physical dimension. The stronger your relationship with the realm, the more likely you are to cultivate a career that's truly aligned with your highest self.

Now go get 'em, rock star!

✦

The deeper
you go,
the higher you climb.

@alizakelly

Next, we'll learn how to face life's biggest challenges with curious compassion, as well as how to convert deep, palpable pain into powerful healing medicine. The upcoming chapter will invite you to explore these topics in comprehensive detail, but I must preface this by acknowledging that—for many readers— this isn't going to be easy. We'll address upsetting themes, including death, depression, drugs, addiction, and infidelity. Before beginning this phase of your journey, take a brief moment to ground yourself with breathwork, supportive pillows, and a few glasses of water. Although these challenging topics are often swept under the rug (both on a personal and societal level), we will soon learn that concealing the tough stuff is counterproductive. Self-actualization requires tenacity, and throughout this chapter, trust that time isn't linear. Within the astral plane everything that will happen—both good and bad—has already occurred. In other words, you already have the courage and fortitude to overcome even the most impossible circumstances. Your bravery is astounding.

SEVEN

THE TOUGH STUFF

"How can I begin to heal my trauma?"

"Why do these cycles continue?"

"When will things get better?"

"Is my life abnormally hard?"

ON PAIN

One of the most extraordinary things about astrology is that it offers a rich language for dealing with hardship. In fact, I think this is the very quality that attracted me to the cosmos: There's solace in the bigger picture—in recognizing that, no matter what impossible situations we're navigating, we're not alone.

Magick exists in the thresholds—the between spaces like doorways, windowsills, twilight, and emotional strife. Rumi (1207–1273), the great Sufi poet, said "the wound is the place where the Light enters you." Likewise, I invite you to explore the warm sunshine as it pours through the fissures of heartbreak, considering the following questions in a journal or your minds' eye.

- When was the last time I checked in with my emotional landscape?

- In what ways have my challenges evolved over time?
- In what ways have my challenges stayed the same?
- When did I last feel as if I needed to avoid confronting the pain?
- When did I last feel as if I could face the pain?
- What helps me align with painful realities?

PAIN MATTERS

I once heard the dead outnumber the living on Facebook. I don't know if that's true. But these days, when someone dies, their social media profile becomes an interactive memorial. We post on their birthday, their death day, and whenever we feel compelled to connect with the dearly departed. These profiles—oddly comforting, macabre time capsules—are a staple of modern bereavement.

In September of 2004, I was just starting my sophomore year of high school and knew nothing about digital graveyards. So it was very strange when, after Landon died, his account was still signed in to AOL Instant Messenger. I suppose, when he was alive, he had attempted to link AIM with his flip phone. But, even as word spread that Landon overdosed on heroin, his screen name continued to appear online. There must have been a glitch in this proto-mobile matrix.

Two days after I found out about his death, I double-clicked his screen name. The message history revealed that we hadn't communicated in over a year.

Landon was my crush in elementary school. In fifth grade—as if by divine intervention—we were seated at the same table; I spent the entire year trying to impress him. I would listen attentively to everything he said, taking note of the bands he liked (Operation Ivy, Slipknot), the activities he enjoyed (skateboarding, graffiti), and the way his eyes lit up (electric blue) when he smiled.

We matriculated into the same middle school and Landon, effortlessly cool, quickly assembled a group of punky, alternative friends, with Landon as leader of the pack. But now I wasn't the only one with a crush: much to my despair, the popular girls also noticed Landon's magnetism and became increasingly vocal about their attraction. I was devastated.

For years, I had curated my entire reality specifically to appeal to Landon's taste—I fused my interests with his interests, steering clear of any trends or fads that didn't mesh with Landon's ethos. But the new members of Landon's fan club had silky straight hair, wore Juicy Couture velour tracksuits, listened to Britney Spears, and spoke in sing-song voices that exuded rich girl confidence. To make matters worse, the feelings were often reciprocal: Despite Landon's edge, he preferred dating preps. Words cannot convey how deeply I resented Avril Lavigne's "Sk8r Boi" (2002) anthem. The lyrics "He was a punk / she did ballet" idealized the very dynamic that was *ruining* my life.

By eighth grade, I had accepted that Landon was not interested in me, so I developed another crush on a Sagittarius named Peter. Peter was two years older, which—at the time—was a massive age difference; he was in *high school*, after all. Unlike Landon, who exuded soulful sensitivity, Peter captured the essence of the Sagittarius archetype: He was confident, fiery, and brutally straightforward.

Peter and I would talk for hours every day on AIM—mostly about music and movies—and, after several weeks, I confessed that I liked him in *that* way. Sadly, Peter did not share that sentiment. In fact—as if doing me a favor—Peter proceeded to list all the reasons he found me unattractive, explicitly dissecting each and every part of my face and body. His observations perfectly aligned with my existing insecurities, confirming that the very same features I criticized in the mirror—my nose, my hair, my stomach, my thighs, my ass—were *actually* problematic.

Clearly, I had to change the way I looked, and, if I wanted love, I also had to adjust my expectations. Maybe sex would change his mind? Maybe after physical touch he would feel emotionally connected to me? Maybe we could build a different type of relationship? It was worth a try.

My first sexual experience with Peter was transactional and traumatic. Later that night, lying in bed, I met an unfamiliar void: nothingness existed in the absence of his presence. The isolation was intolerable, but the passion—that visceral carnality of being *wanted*—was intoxicating. I needed more.

Shortly after my first encounter with Peter, I traded my oversized, tomboy uniform for fishnet stockings and micro-miniskirts, embracing my newfound identity as a self-proclaimed "slut." Scribbling that four-letter word across notebooks, I bragged to my classmates about my promiscuity. Now that I was *sexually experienced* boys were starting to pay attention to me.

One day, I heard through the grapevine that Landon wanted me to give him a blowjob. I could barely contain my excitement. *Me?!* I didn't care *why* Landon was interested, I was just overjoyed he was interested *at all*. Sure, it wasn't exactly the way I imagined—but, by that point, I was hardened enough to know that real life was no fairy tale. It's a cruel world, and now it was time to grow up. Slut was definitely the way to go.

Over AIM, Landon and I made a plan. Landon knew of a small, relatively private courtyard on Seventy-Ninth and East End Avenue, just one block away from school. Should we meet there at lunchtime? No, there would be too many kids around. If we wanted to do this, we would need to cut class in the late morning, right before recess, to avoid running into any teachers or classmates.

"You're not going to back out, right?" Landon asked.

My heart fluttered.

"Of course not," I responded, "I'll see you tomorrow."

The next day, everything went according to plan. Quietly sprinting down the school's back staircase, I pushed the emergency exit open against a cold gust of April wind. Landon was already outside. We walked fast, darting across the street and down the block, avoiding rogue staff and nosey crossing guards. We moved in silence—there was nothing to say.

Landon went into the courtyard first. He looked around, signaled the coast was clear, and sat down on a small bench surrounded by shrubbery. *Had he done this before?* In silence, I kneeled on the gravel—tiny stones pressing into my skin. The rough wind whipped my hair into a tangle. Landon held my head. The sky was overcast. We never kissed.

Landon and I stopped being friends after that. In fact, I'm not sure if we ever spoke again. The encounter was awkward and empty—a bizarre bastardization of my most meaningful childhood crush. I was disappointed in myself for sabotaging any semblance of a relationship and angry at him for reducing me to a mouth.

I never expected an apology—but, a few days after he died, I decided to reach out.

"Are you there?" I typed into the chat box.

I was terrified he would write back. And I was terrified he wouldn't.

He didn't.

But his account remained active: he was online during his funeral. He was online on Halloween—his favorite holiday. He was online when the year changed to 2005, and he was online for the rest of sophomore year. In fact, he remained online throughout all of high school.

As the years went on, his digital presence became less eerie. It was actually comforting: the virtual imprint suggested a sort of otherwordly consciousness. Maybe he wasn't really that far away. Maybe, just on the other side of a screen, he was still quietly growing up.

It's been well over a decade since I used AIM. When I went to college in 2007, I stopped using it entirely, swapping it for a new social media platform called Facebook. So, while I can't say for sure, my sense is that—in the graveyard of forgotten binary code and archaic technology—Landon's still online. Still listening. Still owing me a response.

✖

Astrology is visceral; it's a full sensory experience. Astrology is a 5 A.M. alarm clock, a double shot of cheap tequila, a finger slammed in a dresser drawer. Astrology is as real as it gets—and you *know* shit gets real. Astrology mirrors what you've gone through and validates those experiences with brutal honesty. Nothing is polished or sanded down or buffed out. All your challenges and hardships and secrets and regrets are splayed out right before your eyes, in your 360° birth chart.

Acknowledging your pain is an incredibly empowering experience. We spend so much time running from bad feelings, pretending like trauma *doesn't* compound, but astrology invites a different sort of process: it's not denial, it's recognition. Through the wisdom of the stars, we can embrace challenges as an integral component of being alive. Pain is an electrical current that weaves through all individual and collective experiences.

As I cultivated my relationship with astrology, moving from

student to guide, I discovered how *deeply* I wanted to share astrology's healing properties with others. In fact, the most transformative client sessions are always the most painful ones: I invite clients to get as real as possible during our sessions. So when Olivia asked if we could discuss her infidelity, I told her she'd come to the right place.

Olivia (born December 18, 1984, at 8:26 A.M. in Portsmouth, New Hampshire) met Andrew nine years ago, when she was twenty-six, at a bar in Boston. At that time, Andrew had just started working as a journalist and Olivia was in law school. They were both passionate and fiery and ambitious, so no one was surprised when they got married by the city clerk within less than a year of dating. Not long after that, Olivia became pregnant and they became parents to their only child, Dexter.

Life was happening so fast, she hadn't even stopped to consider if she actually wanted the roles of "wife and mother." As she watched her friends (specifically her male counterparts) become high-powered attorneys, Olivia was stuck at home, cleaning up after her son and husband. She was ashamed to admit it, but the truth was that she resented her situation. Olivia felt trapped.

When Dexter was two, Andrew and Olivia agreed that they could swap roles. Andrew would spend more time at home, and Olivia would return to work. Olivia was hired at a prestigious firm and, like all things in her life, began moving up the ladder rapidly. Her burgeoning career meant more time away from her family, but her salary also made it possible for Andrew to transition to an even lighter freelance schedule.

By the time Dexter was four, Olivia was thriving professionally. Although she was deeply fulfilled by her job, she was worried that people would judge her for prioritizing her career over her family. Olivia became increasingly paranoid, so she gradually stopped mentioning her family at the office and, eventually, decided to stop wearing her wedding ring. She knew Andrew would hate it—so, each morning, when she arrived at work, she would slip the ring off her finger and place it in her wallet, retrieving it only when she would leave to go home. It was sort of like a ritual; a way for her to open and close the workday. She had no dubious intentions, she told me, "It just helped me stay focused."

She did admit, however, that not wearing her ring may have sped things up that night in October—the night she first cheated on Andrew. After a long week, the office got together at a local bar to unwind. The past month had been stressful, so everyone was drinking a bit more heavily than usual, ordering back-to-back rounds of shots.

Olivia's colleagues began dispersing throughout the bar, and the next thing Olivia knew, she was in a spirited conversation with a complete stranger. Tony? Timothy? Tommy? Olivia couldn't remember his name, but she knew he worked at an architecture firm. At some point, they left for another bar, then another, then sloppy kisses on a street corner, then rough sex behind a municipal building in downtown Boston.

Olivia didn't go home that night. After the encounter, she stumbled back to the office where she slept for a few hours. As soon as the building's gym opened, she threw herself into the shower and sobbed. Holy fuck—what had she done?

When she arrived home around 9 A.M. the next morning, the stench of tequila still oozing from her skin, she was prepared to tell Andrew the truth. Olivia would get down on her knees and beg for forgiveness, and explain how she didn't know what came over her, that she would do anything for her family . . . maybe she was spending too much time away from her home . . . she would gladly quit her job.

"I'm so sorry . . ." she started, but before she could even finish her sentence, Andrew kissed her on the head.

"Go get some Advil, you wino," Andrew teased. "Dexter has something to show you, and you're going to hate it."

As Olivia watched her son perform a drum solo on a hand-assembled mound of pots and pans, her mind was racing. *Was Andrew oblivious? Was he in denial? Did he not care? Was he sleeping with other people? Would it even matter now?*

Over the next few weeks, Olivia spent more time at home. At first, she was anxious and paranoid, but eventually, she accepted the fact that Andrew didn't know what had happened that night. No one did. She planned to bury the secret and put it behind her but, not even a year later, the exact same thing happened again—this time, with Eddie from a consulting firm. And then again, nine months later, with Roger the elementary school teacher. She saw Roger a few times, actually; they even spent the night at a hotel together once. And each time Olivia would return home, Andrew and Dexter seemed completely unfazed—as if everything was perfectly normal.

"This isn't normal, right? This isn't okay?" I could hear the tormented desperation in Olivia's voice.

"No, this isn't sustainable," I said. "But everything is going to be okay. We just have work to do."

In my years working as a professional astrologer, I've heard thousands of stories. Likewise, I've helped my clients navigate extraordinarily difficult circumstances. Looking at Olivia's chart, I noted her Sagittarius Sun in the Twelfth House (Plate 8). Astrologers of the past weren't particularly kind to the Twelfth House (but, then again, most antiquated astrology descriptions are quite fatalistic). In my tattered 1967 edition of *A to Z: Horoscope Maker and Delineator* (originally printed in 1910), Llewlyn George describes the Twelfth House as:

". . . representing tribulation, sorrow, and self-undoing, arising from either treachery or persecution of secret enemies, from the bonds of restriction, or from want, poverty, ignorance, or disease. It indicates such things as kidnapping, poisoning, bootlegging, opium trade, smuggling, blackmailing. It rules such places as jails, hospitals, and other institutions of correction and detention, or any enclosure where liberty is curtailed . . . [the] Twelfth House relates to the occult or secret workings of the minds and denotes also schemes, plots, frauds, swindles, intrigue, cabals, conspiracy, or obsession."

Though I wouldn't describe the Twelfth House using *such* inhospitable terms, it's true that this domain does mark a space between worlds. It's in the area of the chart where we prepare to transition from one journey to the next, and likewise, this House is specifically connected to all that exists within the shadows—including death, addictions, and affairs.

Before modern psychology, the Twelfth House was a place riddled with challenges. After all, who would want to move through a domain associated with "self-undoing"? But as our understanding of mental health has expanded, we see that the Twelfth House offers extraordinary insight into the psyche. Yes, we experience many of life's most difficult realities in the Twelfth House—but it's also in this domain that we become aware of our rich multidimensionality. **It is within the Twelfth House that we can learn to grieve, heal, and embrace our profound depths.** As we adjust our eyes to the darkness, it's in the Twelfth House that we can truly comprehend the universe's sprawling sea of stars.

There's a reason life's most challenging circumstances are stored within the Twelfth House. In the final phase of a cycle, we need to courageously confront our pain. Whether you're mourning the death of a relative, the dissolution of a relationship, or simply the culmination of an important chapter of life, you're going to have an emotional experience. **In order to transform pain into power, you must embrace the full extent of your feelings.**

✖

Through time and stars, I've learned that life is just emotions. Your feelings—and your ability to *feel* your feelings—create the structure for daily experiences. This is why, throughout this book, we've been working on both the astral (internal) and physical (external) planes. There's a feedback loop between perception and reality, and in order to self-actualize, we must become active participants in that flow. By now, we've also established that denial is manifestation's mortal enemy. In order to reach your highest purpose, you must lead with veracity. When you actively address a painful situation, you move it out of the shadows and into the light, enabling you to see everything—including your options—more clearly. But when you're up against life's most serious difficulties, it's hard to face the facts. It's easier to numb yourself and pretend that nothing is wrong than to confront the issue head-on.

When you ignore something painful that needs to be addressed, you inadvertently give the problem unchecked power. You see, the issue continues to absorb energy, but now that it's not being monitored, it grows in the darkness. Eventually, this problem becomes a spiritual vacuum, amplifying in intensity, breeding more secrets, and—ultimately—consuming your psyche.

I know it's disgusting, but the best way to visualize this in our Manifestation Café is through a rodent infestation, something I, unfortunately, know a lot about. If there's only one tiny mouse, management may be tempted to ignore the problem, writing it off as an isolated incident and hoping the diners won't notice. However, if this problem goes unaddressed, the mice will begin to multiply. At first, the infestation may only begin on one side of the restaurant, with the rodents quietly running along the wall's perimeter. But without intervention, they will end up consuming the entire restaurant, scampering beneath chairs and tables, horrifying guests and health inspectors alike. Of course, the Manifestation Café cannot continue to operate with these unsanitary conditions; so it shuts down indefinitely (in other words, no internal or external manifestations) until the crisis is properly addressed.

Interestingly, the zodiac sign Scorpio along with its modern planetary ruler, Pluto, are allegorically associated with rodent infestations and plumbing problems, as well as oil, coal, diamonds, and all things that live beneath the surface. The 8th House—the area of the chart associated with sex, death, and transformation—also shares themes with Scorpio and Pluto, representing an area of life that demands deep, emotional exploration. And, because we have all the signs and planets and houses in our individual birth charts, these placements can provide invaluable insight into what shadow means for you.

When looking at Olivia's birth chart, I noticed that her Moon and natal Pluto were conjunct in Scorpio, just a few degrees away from her Midheaven. Pluto is the slowest moving celestial body we track in astrology; it takes 248 years to complete a full orbit (interestingly, the United States will be experiencing its first Pluto Return in February 2022—at the time of this writing, what that means remains to be seen), so we experience Pluto as a "transpersonal planet," meaning its impact is felt on a collective level. People born between November 1983 and November 1995 have Pluto in Scorpio—an astrology signature that corresponds almost perfectly with the Millennial generation. TANC.

Because Pluto is such a distant celestial body, its embodiment comes via aspects to a personal planet. Likewise, Olivia's Moon in Scorpio—representing her emotional inner world—connected to Pluto in Scorpio (symbolizing long-term transformation) conjunct the Midheaven in Scorpio (the highest point in the chart, which showcases long-term legacy) revealed how deeply these transformative themes were in her life.

I also observed that Olivia's Rising Sign[13] was at 13° Capricorn, which meant transiting Pluto in Capricorn (that is, Pluto moving through the sky in real-time) was on her Ascendant between 2014 and 2015. Because Pluto moves so slowly, it's motion across any of the angular houses in our birth charts (1st, 4th, 7th, and 10th Houses) solidifies a cataclysmic transformation in our life associated with the House's function (self, foundation, partnership, legacy, respectively). Through this, I determined that transiting Pluto's movement across her Ascendant activated the Moon-Pluto-Midheaven cluster in her birth chart, exposing the tremendous power of these celestial bodies in her narrative.

Through Olivia's story, it was clear that her compulsive behavior was the physical manifestation of deep, suppressed emotions within the psychic landscape and the longer it was ignored the worse it would get. "Pluto Problems" (a term coined by astrologer Donna Cunningham in her 1986 work, *Healing Pluto Problems*) demand expert intervention, so in addition to metaphysical work, I suggested that Olivia begin working with a therapist—ideally one who specializes in sex and love addiction—as soon as possible.

"Am I going to have to tell Andrew?" Olivia asked.

"Yes, I think it's important for you to know that—eventually—you are going to need to bring this into the light," I continued, "I want you to know, though, that based on what I see in your birth chart, this journey will end up being extremely empowering, and has healing potential beyond your individual reality."

I explained that, often, in the process of mending our deepest wounds, we learn powerful techniques that inspire us to help others. And this insight isn't just for Olivia; it's a universal truth. Ignoring a problem doesn't make it go away: in order to heal, we must face the truth with boundless courage. But, through that tenacity, we uncover unique tools, skills, and expertise—these become our special gifts that we can share with the world.

The adage "hurt people hurt people" is true—if our pain is not addressed and festers in the shadows, we will continue to perpetuate toxic cycles. But, when the tough stuff is brought to the surface, **hurt people heal people,** starting—of course—with themselves.

"Honestly, Olivia, your chart wants to talk about challenging experiences. You're navigating through some choppy waters and it's going to take time, so please be patient with yourself. But I genuinely believe that, on the other side of this, you may end up working with people who are dealing with the exact same issues that you're facing today."

"It's interesting you should say that," Olivia responded, "because I just realized that maybe there's a connection to my mom and her horrible relationship with men. She was always dating the worst guys and constantly moving around with her was extremely stressful. We never talked about how hard that was for me—maybe I should journal about that?"

"Definitely," I said, "that's a great idea."

✳

Self-actualization isn't about stacking your résumé. It's not a laundry list of superlatives, and it's *definitely* not a carefully curated scrapbook of your greatest achievements. Your potential is relative to the scope of your experiences, which includes the joy, sorrow, success, and failure you endure throughout your lifetime. It's true we cannot escape pain—but this emotion also propels us forward. The deeper we go, the higher we climb.

I invite you to embrace the full range of your emotions: the chaotic ones, the jealous ones, the angry ones, the devastating ones. Below are two manifestations (to be performed in the astral plane and physical world, respectively) that will help you begin to navigate the shadows. To truly connect with your emotions is to feel them in their totality. When you accept the full range of your experience—including the tough stuff—you'll be able to make empowered choices that honor your highest purpose. At the end of the day, all the answers you need already exist within. Your strength transcends this lifetime; indeed, it's the backbone of the entire universe.

PAIN REVIEW

- Embracing the full extent of our experiences, including the tough stuff, is an integral step in self-actualization
- Our healing journey begins when we acknowledge our pain
- The Twelfth House helps us understand emotional multidimensionality
- Pluto, Scorpio, and the 8th House invite us to shine light in the shadows

MANIFESTATIONS FOR CHALLENGES

Internal (Astral): The Ball of Yarn

One of the most interesting things about working as a consulting astrologer is that clients are mirrors. I related to Olivia's story—not just because I, too, struggled with sex and love—but because my Rising Sign is 12° Capricorn. And, similarly, Pluto's motion from my 12th House into 1st House marked a tremendous transformation in my life: This was when I finally began confronting the pain I had been working so hard to numb my entire life. Prior to this metamorphosis, I had virtually no emotional regulation. I would muscle my way through objectively difficult situations, showing no sign of vulnerability whatsoever. But then the most minor inconveniences would send me into a tailspin, fueling a complete and total breakdown.

One of the amazing things about astrology is how quickly it calls bullshit—you can never hide from the stars. When I first began seriously studying this practice, my energetic blockages became abundantly clear. I knew I needed to tackle the chaotic mound that was my life, but I had virtually no idea where to start. So I worked from an accessible entry point—a recent heartache that was incredibly distressing. With the help of my mentors, I began tugging on this pain-point, trying to dig up the root. Before I knew it, everything began to unravel. Attached to this seemingly never-ending cord was years upon years of compounded trauma and disappointments and fear and vulnerability. Although I was interfacing as an adult, it was actually my wounded inner child calling the shots. And she needed a lot of love. As each layer revealed itself, it was as if I was comforting that pain for the very first time. It was profound.

This exercise is called **the ball of yarn**—and it's quite literal. To connect with your emotions and explore the depth of this domain, I invite you to untangle a ball of yarn.

First, find an accessible entry point within your mind's eye—this may be an event or experience that triggered a potent emotional response (perhaps it's a recent breakup, or an explosive argument with your sibling, or a financial disappointment at work). Once you've made your selection, find the edge of the yarn and begin tracing it to the core. As your hands move across the thread, note the memories, sensations, and feelings that rise to the surface. You may discover that your untangling is not chronological (perhaps your recent breakup reminds you of your first boyfriend in middle school, which brings up a betrayal you experienced in college, which evokes an argument your parents had when you were nine . . .). Emotions don't abide by the same rules as the material world, so they compound in unexpected ways.

Perfectly poetic, this technique does not have a resolution. Even as you reach the center of the yarn, you'll discover that there's still more—a lot more—that needs to be untangled; this work is a lifelong process. However, this manifestation will help bring awareness to your emotional landscape, enabling you to experience, in real time, the full range of your sensitivities, creating powerful links in the astral plane. Which emotions are familiar? Which are not? Do you observe any themes or patterns? Did any memories surprise you?

This exercise offers a gentle, yet highly impactful, way to cultivate a healthy relationship with your emotions. Don't forget: to live is to feel. Thus, the more we allow ourselves to experience within the astral, the more vibrant life becomes. Since you're here right now, conscious and aware, celebrate the incredible, divine magick of simply existing. It's absolutely miraculous.

External (Physical): Lend a Hand

As a child, I was the last one to fall asleep at sleepovers. It was an agonizing experience.

It always played out the exact same way. At first, my friends would vow to stay awake (sometimes even through a pinky promise)—they would assure me that they're not tired *at all* and, yes, they were ready to "pull an all-nighter." But, at some point during our late night movie watching, I would notice an eerie silence. Lo and behold, I would look over—their face illuminated by the television's glow—and discover their eyes were closed. Usually, I would wake them with a heartfelt cry, "you promised to stay awake!" They would stir for a moment, and respond with those infamous, final words: "I'm just resting my eyes." At that point, I knew the sleepover portion of the evening was over . . . but, unfortunately, my weird and lonely night was just getting started.

The issue wasn't really that I was the last to fall asleep—it was that I was awake for hours and hours and hours. Even now, I can distinctly remember the enveloping solitude. As I tiptoed around my friends' apartments—strange and unfamiliar environments—I felt like I was the only person awake in the entire world. No one could possibly relate to my somber consciousness.

When I'm in the midst of navigating challenges—whether they're emotional, spiritual, or circumstational—I recall this sensation. When you're addressing tough stuff, it's normal to feel completely isolated, like no one could possibly understand your specific pain. And, in a way, that's true: Just like your birth chart, the difficulties you face in this lifetime are uniquely personal.

Your individual challenges may feel so specific to your reality that you might assume no one could understand your breed of sorrow. And pain *coupled* with solitude further magnifies distress, causing your emotions to feel insurmountable, and ultimately, distance yourself from your sensitivities altogether.

But pain is also a shared experience.

No matter who you are or where you come from, you will—at some point in your life—experience profound sorrow. While there are some journeys that are objectively "harder" than others, your perception of reality solely exists within the scope of your consciousness. In many ways, pain is a universal language.

Perhaps R.E.M. said it best: *Everybody hurts sometimes.*

This technique, which I've titled **lend a hand**, is an external manifestation designed to help you connect with the full range of your emotions. In order to perform this exercise, you need to expand your perspective by offering support to others in need. Volunteering at a food pantry, after-school programs, retirement facility, or correctional center is a great way to actualize this technique.

One of the reasons I love this manifestation is because your personal experiences remain entirely intact. No matter how you're currently managing your sensitivities, this exercise invites you to explore another, entirely separate, dimension of feeling. It broadens your vantage, allowing you to process your emotions on both a micro (personal) and macro (collective) level.

Further, your sensitivities actually become a conduit for compassion, closing the loop on an even cosmic greater exploration. Astrology (and, accordingly, consciousness) is a practice in empathy. By aligning with your own emotional landscape, you create a bridge to cycles that extend past your vantage.

Whether or not you're currently facing a challenge, lending a hand is a wonderful way to deepen your connection to the emotional landscape. Rather than feel stifled by your complicated sensitivities, this manifestation proves that feelings transcend reality. Yes, your emotions might be messy and chaotic and uncomfortable—but it's only through these intense sensations that you can support others, tapping into the greater good and, likewise, the collective consciousness. Through this exercise, you can see how your personal truths are neatly folded into the fabric of humanity, binding us to fellow stargazers of the past, present, and future. Your emotions are, in fact, your pathway into the universe. Relish the expanse.

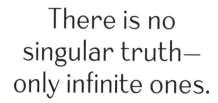

There is no
singular truth—
only infinite ones.

@alizakelly

EIGHT

COSMIC INTUITION

"What can I do to cultivate my intuition?"

"I'm an empath—does that mean I'm psychic?"

"How do I manage big feelings?"

"What if I see a ghost?"

ON INTUITION

Astrology can be extremely technical. The stars and planets can be explored from a purely mathematical perspective; coordinates and geometry and horoscopes delineated with clinical precision. When I was younger, I felt anchored by the logic of astrology, as if its tangibility justified the practice, but space void of emotion is astronomy—a critical science—that's distinctive from this practice. Through time, I found that astrology is animated through mysticism: Astrology is a portal into deep, complex, and transformative spirituality. The cosmos can enhance your existing religiosity, or cultivate an entirely new connection with the sublime. As a secular practitioner, astrology has empowered me to trust my intuition, strengthen my psychic abilities, and find meaning in consciousness. As you begin this final chapter, consider what spirituality means to you in a journal or your mind's eye. There are no right or wrong answers—let your responses flow through you like seasons. You are, after all, an extension of nature. Give yourself permission to transform.

- When did I last check in with my intuition?
- In what ways has my intuition changed over time?
- In what ways has my intuition stayed the same?
- When did I last feel like I could understand my intuition?
- When did I last feel as if I couldn't understand my intuition?
- What helps me align with my intuition?

INTUITION MATTERS

Congratulations, you've now reached the final phase in this journey. Now, it's time to synthesize all that you've learned and extend your practice even further. This chapter is about connecting the dots to create your own beautifully illuminated constellations, identifying the unique star clusters that exist within your reality and, indeed, destiny.

While all of our lives—all of our experiences—are individual, they're also all embedded within the cycles of our collective consciousness. Every single person plays a pivotal role in the energetic flow of existence. And just as the Babylonians projected themselves into the stars, etching their existence into eternity, we use astrology to understand our own limitless magick. Your consciousness has no boundaries; just as the astral plane is perpetually expanding, you can choose—if you so desire—to stretch your reality as far as you can dream.

The most important principle of astrology—or any metaphysical practice, for that matter—is embedded in the powerful Hermetic axiom:

As Above, So Below
As Within, So Without

In other words, everything that exists in one realm of reality also occurs in another. Of course, you've already been working with this adage throughout your manifestation practice. Your ideas in the astral plane *become* your reality in the physical world. In fact, these dimensions coexist in such perfect harmony that you must be extraordinarily diligent about not just what you do, but what you *absorb* because—even when you don't realize it—external stimuli is constantly shaping your experiences on an energetic level.

In a birth chart, there are many different placements that could indicate psychic power but, like all things in astrology, the planets alone cannot determine whether someone does or doesn't have extrasensory abilities. Usually, the presence of extrasensory gifts is easiest to spot through the conversation itself.

Zarina was a bit anxious about our first session—I told her that was totally normal and, even today, I sometimes *still* get nervous when one of my teachers looks at my birth chart. It makes you feel very vulnerable. "Plus," I said, "you may think I'm going to tell you something scary."

"Exactly!" Zarina exclaimed.

"But don't worry, that's not how astrology works—at least, that's not the type of astrology I practice. Astrology is agency, it's free will. What I'm going to offer you, through your chart, is perspective. We're going to see how the planets line up with your reality and, from there, we'll be able to understand how certain events or themes relate to even broader cycles. Does that make sense?"

She said yes, and we continued forward.

Zarina (born June 29, 1993, at 5:03 P.M. in El Paso, Texas) was gentle and soft-spoken. Weaving through her birth chart, I observed different dimensions of her personality, family relationships, and her deeply sensitive spirit (Plate 9). I asked her how often she works with her intuition.

Zarina sighed and said, "I hate my intuition."

I've heard *lots* of wild stories as an astrologer, but I'd never heard someone say they flat-out *hate* their intuition. I asked Zarina to explain.

"Well, whenever I have a feeling about something, it always turns out to be trouble."

Zarina told me that when she was a kid, she knew her house was haunted because, each time she walked into her bedroom, her pillows would be flipped over, facing the other direction. But when she decided to tell her mom about it, Zarina's mother told her to stop making things up. And then, not long after, she was looking out her window and saw her father get into a strange car; there was a woman driving. So, again, Zarina told her mom—only this time, her mom was even more hurtful; she called Zarina a "fucking liar."

So Zarina stopped telling her mom the things that happened in the house (the flickering lights, the weird noises, the pungent smells) and the things that happened outside of the house (her father leaving in the middle of the night, her father stumbling into the house drunk, her father getting violent with his brother). Zarina didn't want to upset her mother. So she started keeping secrets.

Zarina had even more stories about premonitions. She knew when her best friend was pregnant. She even knew when her apartment got burgled. And she even knew when her grandmother was going to die.

"Zarina," I said, "it sounds like you might be psychic."

Zarina laughed. "No way—I just know shit."

There's a lot of stigma attached to the word "psychic." For many of us, it seems to imply shady, unethical business dealings. I remember my first interaction with a storefront psychic: I was about four or five years old and I was walking with my parents on Broadway—we must have been returning home from dinner because it was dark. Always unapologetically independent, I ran about thirty feet ahead so I could pretend to be strolling by myself.

My senses were heightened; I was a city kid, so I knew danger lurked behind every corner. I had to be careful and never, ever talk to strangers. But when a boy about my age scampered over to say hello, I returned the salutation. Adults are dangerous, but kids are safe—right?

"Do you want to play?" he asked, and pointed to a building just about ten feet away. Two steps down, just slightly below street level, neon violet light—such a distinct early 1990s hue—flooded onto the street through large, clean glass windows.

I have a faint memory of a floor-to-ceiling mirror, black faux-leather chairs, and wallpaper with an antiqued patina. Then, I remember my mom yelling my name and my dad swooping me up. Yes, I was in trouble for wandering off—but I was also told that those types of places were trouble.

Eventually I learned the meaning of that glowing signage—PSYCHIC—and began to associate that word with danger. For many years, the only time I encountered that word was when I saw it radiating from a shop window. So, even as I began to explore astrology in my early twenties, I was still quick to raise an eyebrow at anything potentially "psychic."

As I became increasingly committed to the metaphysical

domain, I learned that manifestations only materialize through full and complete honesty. After all, you can't get what you want unless you're willing to *admit* what you want. But that wasn't all. This transparency wasn't just about acknowledging truths in the physical realm, but also truths within the astral sector: truths that existed purely within intuition. Our psychic powers.

Although we may interpret "psychic powers" through the lens of "New Age" spirituality, our extrasensory abilities are actually embedded within our DNA—they're survival instincts. Just as other animals use their myriad senses to detect danger, humans also use a host of skills to make sense of their surroundings, scanning for any potential threats. External senses—sight, sound, smell, taste, and touch—help us understand the tangible world, but there are also emotional senses that help us process the truths that exist beyond the physical sector. Intuition is your birthright. Intuition is constantly flowing between the physical dimension and the astral plane, revealing critical insight that has the ability to not just inform, but also amplify your manifestation practice. Likewise, the final—albeit perhaps most important—aspect of self-actualizing is tapping into your innate psychic abilities.

When it comes to intuition and spirituality, I look to Neptune. **Neptune, the distant planet that spins at the edge of our solar system, represents imagination, creativity, and fantasy, along with all that cannot be explained.** Named after the mythological god of the sea (Poseidon in Greek folklore), Neptune operates on hydraulics, using water (a symbol of the unknown) to generate transformation. Neptune's magick is imbued with thick fog, which, in the right circumstance (say, a misty stroll through the park), can be enchanting and romantic.

However, in the wrong conditions (for instance, when driving on a windy cliff at night), Neptune's opacity is terrifying—even deadly. Neptune swallows boundaries and limitations and rationality. Without the confines of structure, however, psychic wisdom must be anchored to a different set of principles: inspiration, compassion, and integrity are the pillars of transcendence.

Believe it or not, psychic powers are (most of the time) not that mind-blowing. To have psychic abilities means you have sensory abilities that go beyond the normal boundaries of the physical realm. Defining "normal boundaries," however, is a whole other issue. How do we know whether our senses are more pronounced than others? After all, we're conditioned to believe that the world around us is standard: you may assume that everyone visualizes the sky as the same shade of blue, or that the smell of cinnamon always generates nostalgia, or that you can detect someone's mood through the sound of their footsteps. But that's not the case.

Just as each individual has a different reality, each individual also has different intuitive gifts. Some people receive psychic data through physical objects, such as holding an energetically-charged crystal or a possession that belonged to a loved one. Others may "download" etheric insight from images (like looking at a photograph), and still others might experience a powerful sense of "knowing" that adds deep dimensionality to day-to-day situations. In fact, *because* everyone has such different experiences within the world, we will never know all the ways we can experience psychic gifts.

Because extrasensory gifts can be so different from person to person, a better way of gauging your psychic abilities is by learning the "strength" of your individual gifts. To do this, it's best to imagine your abilities on a spectrum. To visualize this spectrum, imagine four friends meeting for dinner at . . . you guessed it. Your favorite esoteric restaurant: the Manifestation Café.

When the first friend, Ashley, arrives, she walks over to the host, gives her name to the *maître d'*, and is escorted to the table reserved for her party. Once Ashley sits down, she realizes that she's super thirsty—fortunately, there's a bottle of tap water already on the table, so she fills her glass and takes a sip.

Next, the second friend, Bobbi, arrives, at the restaurant. As soon as Bobbi steps through the door, she notices that the *maître d'* is intently focused on her phone: scrolling through Instagram, taking screenshots, texting friends. Bobbi wonders if the host is usually this distracted? Or did something happen? But in just a matter of seconds, the *maître d'* notices Bobbi and welcomes her to the restaurant. They make their way to the table, where Bobbi sits down, greets Ashley, and proceeds to review the menu.

Shortly after, the third friend—Cathy—arrives at the restaurant. Before she even reaches the host stand, she's overloaded with information about her environment: the *maître d'* is on her phone, the servers keep bumping into each other, and someone is speaking obnoxiously loud. Cathy locates the voice—a man at a table with four other individuals, all wearing suits. Cathy determines it must be a business meeting. *Is he always that overbearing?* she wonders. Suddenly, the *maître d'* says hello and Cathy is snapped back into reality. Cathy gives the name of the dinner reservation and the *maître d'* escorts her to the table.

"Hey guys," Cathy says, sitting down. "Do you hear that guy over there? He's so inconsiderate . . ."

Neither of them had noticed before, but yes—now that it's mentioned, he is quite loud.

Finally, the fourth friend, Dora, walks into the restaurant.

The moment Dora enters, she's overwhelmed with stimuli: movement, sound, lights, smells. Instantly, she feels the energy of every single guest, the complex dynamics within the restaurant staff, the distinctive aroma of a pungent dish that reminds Dora of her aunt's cooking, and a few charred beams on the ceiling. All in lightning speed, Dora connects with the energy of the space and feels a wave of sadness wash over her—*yes, there was once a fire in this building.* Dora doesn't want to interact with the *maître d'* while she's on her phone (Dora can tell she's gossiping about someone), so she bypasses the host stand and hurries toward her friends.

"Hi, Dora! Are you okay? You look a little upset," Cathy asks, pouring water into her glass. Dora says she's fine and apologizes for being late.

In the above example, Ashley and Bobbi demonstrate a "normal" range of sensitivity. Ashley's experience is driven by her perception, so the stimuli she receives is directly connected to her own, immediate needs. Bobbi reveals a slightly more nuanced response to her environment (for instance, contemplating the reason behind the host's incessant phone use), but the observations are still shaped by her specific agenda.

Cathy and Dora, on the other hand, exhibit much higher levels of sensitivity. Cathy's awareness transcends her own reality, as she notices details in her surroundings that exist beyond her immediate narrative. Although Cathy is hyperaware, she's able to integrate these abilities into the physical realm. In fact, she even expands upon her peers' sensitivities, which invites them to become more receptive.

Dora's psychic sensitivites are all-consuming. Through her powerful awareness she was reacting not just to circumstances within her immediate environment (such as the arrogant businessman), but also those that exist within alternative dimensions. Inundated with stimuli, boundaries between realms blur: Dora's dining experience is more nuanced than simply catching up with friends.

I would identify both Cathy and Dora as having innate psychic abilities. Simply, this means that there is an organic flow between the astral and physical realms, which informs their perception of reality. This, however, doesn't mean that Ashley and Bobbi are *void* of psychic skills; perhaps their intuition wasn't fired off in that particular circumstance, or perhaps they've learned to manage their psychic input to make mundane activities—like entering a restaurant—emotionally uneventful experiences.

As learning how to manage your extrasensory abilities integrates the astral and physical realms, this is truly the final phase of self-actualization. By harnessing your unique gifts, you'll discover how every single domain is inextricably linked. By working with our psychic powers, we can begin to connect the dots.

Stabilizing your psychic sensitivities will enable you to pick up on important, subtle details without becoming totally overloaded by excessive energetic data. Cultivating your unique psychic abilities—ensuring they're working *for* you as opposed to *against* you—is essential spiritual hygiene. But like all aspects of this self-actualization process, working with your intuition requires active awareness.

Through my one-on-one work with clients, I've discovered that it's quite common to feel like your psychic abilities are "broken." Perhaps you're totally disconnected from your intuition? Or maybe you don't know how to regulate the constant flood of energetic information you receive through your psychic channels? I'm thrilled to report that your innate sensory gifts can be fine-tuned and, just like all topics covered in this book, compassionate curiosity is the first step in this process.

✶

Most people develop their psychic abilities during child-hood. Occasionally, a deeply intuitive individual (a relative or close confidant) will teach us how to work with our intuition, helping us form thoughtful connections between our extra-sensory experiences and the physical world. But while devel-oping your intuition with a trusted mentor is wonderful, it is—unfortunately—quite rare. The majority of us develop our gifts as a *reaction* to environmental conditions. Embedded in the foundation of our consciousness, we establish bonds between the physical and non-physical realms.

During our formative years, we have no real responsibilities, but we also have no real freedom. Just as we don't choose our family, we cannot choose our circumstances. Likewise, we de-velop intuitive skills so that we can adapt to our surroundings. As young children, we notice more, see more, hear more, and feel more. You can anticipate your father's mood by the sound of his voice, or know if your mother is upset based on the way her lip curls, or if your older sister is getting into trouble based on the smell of her perfume. As we start to create correlations between subtle details and feelings, your innate hyperaware-ness transforms into extrasensory skills that offer insight into the unique feedback loops that shape your reality.

It's through these conditions that people often become "em-paths." Here, it is important to note the distinction between exercising empathy and *being* an empath. When we practice empathy, we choose to relate to others on an emotional level—empathy *requires* agency. Empaths, on the other hand, are indi-viduals who absorb others' emotions as a way to *simulate* agency.

Likewise, many empaths are the byproducts of chaotic, hostile, or confusing environments. Environments where—in order to understand *why* your mom was drinking or your dad was absent or you were constantly being criticized—you had to form deep emotional connections in order to make sense of your reality.

Interestingly, it's here that we can also note the fascinating correlation between empaths and narcissists[14]—as they coexist on the same axis. The challenging circumstances that drive someone to dial up their sensitivities so high that they *embody* another person's internal experience, thus becoming an empath, can also cause the same individual to exhibit narcissism: to demand emotional control, to feed off energetic power, and to build walls as soon as someone gets too close.

So, although modern mystics praise empaths for "feeling" and vilify narcissists for "manipulating," these conditions are ultimately two sides to the same coin—just as every zodiac sign has its opposite, these two expressions of intuition are inextricably linked. Depending on the situation, the empath can become the narcissist, or the narcissist can become the empath. If you identify with these qualities, emotional regulation is essential, and this can be achieved by strengthening your spiritual hygiene through daily practices and rituals, along with working with experts in psychology and spirituality.

It should be noted that your childhood didn't need to be exceptionally traumatic for you to develop these skills. As an adult, you know how horrific and dysfunctional some upbringings can be, which—by comparison—could make your experience seem idyllic. But, when you're a kid, you don't have that perspective. Your reality is merely a construction of your consciousness, which means your extrasensory skills were cultivated to reflect your *individual* perspective. So, even if you now recognize that your early years were relatively normal, your intuition is still structured around your individual experiences: noticing the way the sun felt on your skin when your mom was late to pick you up from school, or how your dad avoided eye contact when he couldn't attend your dance recital, or how you got nauseous right before your parents started bickering in the car.

✹

Extrasensory abilities are part of human evolution. Your intuition is real. It's always been real. But, to make matters even more complicated, we receive feedback that challenges our psychic abilities:

"You're too sensitive."
"That's your imagination."
"Nothing's wrong—everything's fine."

Likewise, we're conditioned to believe that only tangible truths have value. We're taught that ghosts are pretend, pain is physical, and psychic abilities are just an illusion. These messages contradict our innate intuition and, subsequently, distort our gifts. For instance, Zarina's mother not only denied her psychic abilities, but also ridiculed her for possessing them in the first place. Likewise, Zarina had a strained relationship with her intuition. It's no surprise that, for Zarina, these extrasensory abilities felt like more of a curse than a blessing.

Now, because intuition is a function of survival skills, it's true that psychic feelings often indicate trouble. But extrasensory abilities are more than just "red flags." **For many of us, the first step to tapping into psychic skills is simply accepting that these gifts are, indeed, both real and complex**. Your psychic senses are an honest extension of your reality and, once you fortify a relationship with your intuition, your profound sense of knowing will apply to both positive and negative situations. Yes, you may be alerted to danger—but you'll also connect with joy and adoration and opportunity. You'll know when you're moving in the right direction, and you'll know when you've aligned with your highest potential. Because, at the end of the day, your psychic abilities respond to the reality that *you* created for *yourself,* and these extrasensory gifts are as tangible as any object that exists in the physical realm. Even when others don't understand your psychic feedback loop, you will always know what it means.

Accordingly, another major psychic blockage occurs when we expect others to validate our intuition. We may try to identify causation—proof that our extrasensory observations detected something rooted in reality—but it's unlikely we'll receive that confirmation. For instance, hindsight reveals that Zarina's mother was clearly buried in denial, so acknowledging Zarina's intuition would force her to face facts she was unwilling to accept. A child, however, cannot unpack this multilayered, psychological nuance, so instead, they experience shame and guilt for expressing their sensitivities.

Unfortunately, this doesn't just end in childhood: even as we mature, we won't always be able to substantiate our psychic feelings on an interpersonal level. Sometimes, even if we never receive palpable proof, we need to trust our gut fully and completely.

I was lucky enough to learn this lesson firsthand in 2009, during my semester abroad. While I was studying in Rome, I started "dating" (whatever that means when you're twenty) another guy in my program—his name was Kyle and he was from Pittsburgh. About three weeks after we first referred to each other as "boyfriend and girlfriend," both Kyle and I left Rome for separate weekend plans: I was meeting a friend in Prague and Kyle was going on a class trip to Brussels. Back in those days, smartphones were still relatively rare and—because international data rates were so expensive—most of us American students weren't using cell phones. So when Kyle and I said goodbye to each other on Friday morning, there was no expectation that we would be in contact until we saw each other back in Rome on Sunday night.

When I met my friend Sammy in Prague, we spent the whole night talking about our programs, our new friends, and our study abroad romances. I was super excited about Kyle—I told Sammy how much fun we were having and how we had just become an official "item" a few weeks prior. That night, I bought him a little souvenir at a gift shop, a decorative bottle opener. So adorable.

The next morning, however, I felt a bit . . . off. I couldn't identify what shifted; it wasn't that I was tired or hungover, I just felt strange. I didn't let it spoil my day—Sammy and I had a terrific afternoon filled with back-to-back adventures, but I found myself increasingly less interested in talking about Kyle. By the evening, I didn't want to bring him up at all.

"Did something happen with Kyle?" Sammy asked as we were finishing dinner.

"No, of course not," I snapped. "I haven't talked to him."

As the night continued, I became increasingly anxious. As Sammy and I darted from bar to bar, my bad feelings continued to swell. At one point, I remember taking Kyle's gift out of my purse—I'd changed my mind and I didn't want him to have it anymore. I intentionally left it in a bathroom as I fixed my makeup in the mirror. By the time Sammy and I made our way back to the hostel, I was fighting back tears.

Sammy's flight was early in the morning, so we woke up, had a quick breakfast, and said goodbye before she left for the airport. As soon as I was alone, I started sobbing. I sobbed as I headed for the airport and I sobbed as I boarded the plane.

I sobbed when my flight landed and I sobbed as I hailed a cab back to the residence hall.

As soon as I got to my apartment, I called my friend Josie using the old-fashioned rotary landline in my quirky apartment that hadn't been renovated since the mid-1970s. She answered right away.

"Hi Josie, it's Aliza." My voice trembled. "Can you come over? I'm really upset and I don't know why."

"Yes, absolutely." Her voice was comfortingly efficient. "I'll be there in two minutes."

I swung open the front door as soon as I heard her footsteps on the stairs. Mascara was streaming down my cheeks and Josie wrapped her arms around me in a tight embrace.

"I'm so sorry," she exhaled.

It was so nice to have my feelings validated . . . but wait . . . *what?* I stepped back, leaving Josie's arms suspended in midair.

"What are you sorry about?" I asked.

Josie's arms dropped to her sides. She took a step back, too. "Well, why are you crying?" she asked.

"I don't know why I'm crying—I've just felt horrible all weekend," I responded, and watched as she shot her hand up to her face, covering her mouth. "What happened, Josie?"

"I . . . I . . . I thought you knew because you were crying . . ."

"*Knew what?* What happened, Josie?" I pressed again.

"Well . . . Kyle promised he would tell you, so I guess I might as well . . ."

My heart sank.

"Aliza, he cheated on you."

Josie refused to say any more, so I walked over to the ivory rotary phone and dialed Kyle's room. I wasn't sure if he was back from his trip yet, but when he answered, I told him to meet me in the dorm's courtyard. So I washed my face, put on a fresh layer of makeup, and headed downstairs.

The moment I saw him, I knew he was going to lie: he wore a huge grin and was carrying a box of Belgian chocolates—my souvenir gift. Kyle proceeded to tell me how much he'd missed me and how stupid his trip was and how he was so lonely . . . suffice it to say, he was caught off guard when I asked him for details about Saturday night. And to explain what *the fuck* he was thinking when he decided to fuck someone else.

At first, he denied it. He went on a long diatribe about his morals and virtues and how he wasn't a cheater. And then, after what felt like hours, he redirected his anger toward Josie. "How could she fucking tell you? She has no right!"

I told Kyle that Josie *didn't* tell me—I knew, from afar. I knew on Saturday morning that he was flirting with someone, and I knew on Saturday night when it actually happened. He said he didn't believe me; what, I could just *feel* something was wrong? We hadn't even been in contact! I couldn't have known that.

But I didn't need to convince Kyle; his opinion on the whole situation didn't matter (I mean, I was *obviously* breaking up with him). The truth was that I knew what happened based solely on my intuition. My psychic sense was so powerful that I was already lamenting the end of the romance before I received the tangible evidence of his deceit.

It didn't take me long to understand the value of this experience. Should the situation have not unfolded in that precise order—if I hadn't called Josie crying, or if Josie wasn't aware of Kyle's cheating—I would never have known the truth. Kyle would've pretended like nothing ever happened and all those horrible feelings I had in Prague would've never been explained. Thankfully, TANC. Even that night, as I told the story to the rest of my study-abroad friends, I felt a profound lightness. I knew that I no longer needed to second-guess my intuition; I knew my psychic gifts would never let me down.

✖

Your extrasensory knowledge will always support you. But does that mean that, each time you get a bad feeling, you're about to get dumped? Or fired? Or—God forbid—get into an accident? No, no, no. Not at all. You see, another very common psychic blockage occurs when we conflate intuition with anxiety. Simply put, **anxiety isn't intuition**. Although they may appear similar at first, anxiety and intuition are two totally different energetic experiences. Fortunately, once you know how to distinguish these sensations, it's easy to separate them within your own life.

Psychic insight arrives unexpectedly. In fact, intuition may seem somewhat random. It strikes out of nowhere and rolls through your consciousness in bursts or waves. What's particularly notable about intuition is that the messages often appear through sensory channels. Even when you become fluent in your psychic language, intuition will attach itself to colors, sounds, smells, tastes, or textures. Intuition can be a tightness in your hips or the color blue or an old song that seems to pop into your head out of nowhere. No matter how familiar you become with your psychic gifts, there will always be a magical, codified quality to these experiences.

Like a predator imitating the call of its prey, anxiety mimics the revelatory nature of intuition. Unlike intuition, however, anxiety doesn't just appear out of nowhere—it occurs in response to a high-pressure situation. Anxiety is a reaction, not a premonition.

For instance, imagine you just sent a vulnerable, honest text to your crush. Usually, they responds quickly . . . but right now, it's taking them a lot longer than usual to reply. You may start second-guessing your text, reading it and rereading it again to make sure that you didn't say anything that could be misinterpreted. *Did the message go through? Did they get it? Did they hate it? Do they hate me?* In this chaotic moment, you wonder if your intuition is signaling a major problem. Are you having a psychic moment?

No—intuition wouldn't appear in these hostile conditions; that destructive, circular thinking is fear *disguising* itself as knowing. To be perfectly honest, the blaring siren of anxiety will always overpower the gentle hum of intuition. As the anxious mind churns through every possible worst-case scenario, it wedges out any room for psychic discovery.

Throughout this book, you've discovered that you are a complete cosmology. In our exploration of the stars, we see how your reality mirrors the expanse of the universe—and vice versa. Within this beautiful metaphysical solar system, microcosms and macrocosms cascade onto one another, each nestled perfectly within these limitless cosmic cycles. And bolstering all of these intricate systems is a tightly woven web of energy.

In your physical body, every muscle, bone, nerve, artery, vein, and internal organ (including the heart, lungs, brain, and spinal cord) is encased by fascia—a thin layer of connective tissue that, quite literally, holds you together. This continuous web of collagen fibers exists from head to toe without interruption, forming an anatomical network that links every unique, individual body part to create a collective whole. Messages flow through fascia, carrying experiences from one space to another: a biological depiction of energy moving in real time.

The concept of a flowing life force appears in cultures throughout the world: *Qi* in traditional Chinese medicine, *prana* in Hindu philosophy, and *ka* in ancient Egyptian religion. These names describe the essence of life, a powerful current that animates all natural things—within my astrological practice, I refer to this as energy. Energy electrifies fascia beneath your skin, eye contact on a first date, inky waves of the ocean, and asteroids blasting through space. Energy activates everything you can see, as well as everything you *can't* see; it illuminates all of our planes of existences.

Manifestations help us connect with energy on both an astral (internal) and physical (external) level. By establishing an active role in your consciousness, you identify, harness, and direct your energy toward your highest purpose. Of course, it's important to note that the outcome of your manifestation will always reflect your reality—likewise, honesty and transparency are absolutely essential as you approach each area of life with dynamic awareness. In order to create the life you want, you need to first acknowledge what you desire.

But of course, your manifestations don't exist within a silo. And it's for this reason that your psychic abilities play such a critical role in your journey toward self-actualization. By formulating a rich language with your intuition, you know how to shift your energy to maximize your potential. Ultimately, your extrasensory gifts serve as intermediaries enabling you to make better, more thoughtful choices that align with your core truths. Accordingly, the more you become aware of how you connect with your broader environment, the easier it will be for you to identify the clearest route to self-actualization.

Don't worry—even if blockages have warped your intuition, your extrasensory gifts are part of your cosmic (and human) DNA, which means even the most knotted intuition can be untangled. Though it may require a bit of work, here are two wonderful, time-honored techniques to help you tap into your psychic skills. Your intuition is like a muscle: the more you use it, the stronger it becomes, and the more confident you'll feel in its ability. When you align with yourself as a 360° cosmic body, you'll discover that your authentic self—just like the 360° zodiac and the birth chart and the life cycle—is fully and completely whole. When you connect with your psychic abilities, you unlock the power to embrace the divine magic of simply being you.

INTUITION REVIEW

- Intuition and psychic abilities are an innate part of consciousness
- Anxiety manifests differently than intuition—through practice, these can be differentiated
- Astrology is animated through soul, spirit, and magick
- Neptune is a portal into spirituality, which builds wisdom or compassion

INTUITION MANIFESTATIONS

Internal (Astral): Color Coordination

Imagine you're scrolling through your favorite social media platform and, suddenly, you stumble onto a vaguely familiar name. Could this be . . . why, yes, it is! It's that old friend from childhood you've been thinking about, like, *forever!* Excited, you shoot them a message and ask if they also remember you.

"Yes, of course!" they enthusiastically respond.

You chat back and forth for a moment; you're both so thrilled to reconnect. Quickly, you realize you're in the same city, so you make plans to meet up for coffee later in the week. As the days go by, you eagerly await your meetup. You can't wait to reminisce and share childhood stories. You wonder if they'll be able to unlock long-lost memories. Even now, you can so distinctly remember your old dynamic, the way you bounced creative ideas off each other so effortlessly.

Finally, the day arrives. You skip to the café, and—as discussed—wait for your friend by the front entrance. But as soon as you see each other, you realize how much time has gone by. It's true, a lot has changed since your last playdate: your friend isn't a little kid anymore, they're an adult . . . just like you. As you sit down and start chatting, you also realize that these shifts are more than just physical. Although you're both the same people, you've lived such different lives, and these experiences have had a profound influence on your respective identities. Yes, your old friend is familiar—their laugh is exactly the same—but in most ways, you two are now complete strangers. You realize that if you want to build a friendship, you're going to need to start from scratch.

This scenario is exactly like the process of reconnecting with your psychic abilities. Whether you've lost touch with intuition or feel like your psychic abilities are always misfiring, you want to take time to consciously meet your extrasensory gifts in the here and now. Treat your intuition like this old childhood friend: of course, it's still recognizable—after all, it's been part of your spirit since day one—but in order to cultivate a healthy, functional relationship in the present moment, you need to be willing to start from the ground up.

This exercise is going to help you establish a solid baseline for your psychic abilities. This reflective technique for the astral (internal) realm is called **color coordination**—it's super easy, and as you're strengthening your intuitive muscle, I recommend practicing once daily.

To begin, visualize a recent, straightforward emotional experience. For instance, you can recall an aggravating meeting with your least favorite co-workers or a sexy late-night text exchange with your new lover. Now, choose colors to associate with these experiences and their corresponding feelings (in this example, let's select yellow and pink, respectively). As you imagine each scenario, flash that color in your mind's eye as if you're putting a filter over the scene. Repeat this enough times so that, when you reflect on the scenario, the entire memory is washed in its associated hue.

Now, choose two more scenarios that prompted similar emotional reactions. Perhaps a disagreement with your landlord also exudes yellow, and the memory of romantic physical intimacy illuminates pink. Practice the same visualization as before, blasting this color across the memory so that the two senses become intertwined.

Ultimately, what you've doing is creating a link between color and emotion, enabling you to formulate a direct line of contact to your intuition. Once you're consciously created a correspondence between a color and an emotional energy (in this example, we've identified yellow as annoyance and pink as romance), your psychic abilities will be able to signal events that exist outside of the immediate, physical realm. So, if you see yellow when your supervisor shoots you an email asking for a quick chat you'll know that this dialogue will be sure to spark frustration . . . or if you see pink when your best friend tells you that she has a new neighbor, you'll know she's thinking about them romantically.

Through practice, this color coordination technique can become a powerful manifestation to channel your psychic powers. By getting to know your intuition and developing a fluid, nonverbal language, you can use your extrasensory gifts to make inspired choices that support your highest purpose.

Physical (External): Remote Control

Although psychic abilities are rooted within the intangible astral plane, you can also access your intuition through the tangible, material world. As with all areas of life, it's best to have multiple entry points just in case one dimension feels a bit congested or inaccessible. Likewise, you can enter your extrasensory world through a practice called **remote control**.

This is one of my favorite manifestation techniques because it grounds an etheric concept within reality. In order to perform this technique, all you need to do is select an object that you can keep in your pocket or purse. This object can have metaphysical roots (like a crystal or talisman) or it could be an everyday article (such as a button or penny)—ultimately, the prescribed mystical "worth" of any object is at your sole discretion, as it is simply a conduit for your own innate power. Indeed, even the most seemingly enchanted tool is only magick because you deem it to be. So, for this technique, choose an object that feels exciting and dynamic (and that you won't lose), but don't feel obligated to invest in something you don't already own.

Next, we're going to turn this object into your psychic remote control. In order to do this, we'll need to first calibrate it by identifying an "on" and "off" button. These could be the front and back, the top and bottom, or—like with many television remotes—this could even be a single button that toggles between two modes. Wherever you assign these on the object, make sure you make sure you consciously decide that "on" means your channels are open to psychic messages, while "off" means you're not receiving any energetic stimuli.

Carry this newly programmed remote control in your pocket, wallet, or purse, and practice flipping between these modes in various situations. If you switch this to "on" before an important pitch, will your psychic abilities help you gain deeper insight into what your prospective clients are looking for? Or, if you switch your remote control to "off" before stepping onto a crowded city bus, will you be able to have a (relatively) peaceful ride that allows you to reflect on your day? Do you move through the world differently when you have the ability to take ownership of your intuition?

Because the remote control is simply a physical extension of your own intuitive power, you can eventually remove the object from the technique as you toggle between "on" and "off" in your mind's eye. Fundamentally, this manifestation is a practice in agency. Although it may seem like our psychic abilities exist independently from our consciousness, our extrasensory abilities are also an extension of our reality. When we practice working with our intuition in a healthy, productive way, it can become a functional tool in our journey toward self-actualization. By creating your psychic abilities, you reclaim agency of your intrinsic gifts and send a powerful message to the universe that you are ready to live your best life.

✦

The wisdom
of the black holes
is that they are, too, whole.

@alizakelly

NINE

MORE THAN THIS

Whether you've digested this book at the speed of light or cautiously combed through each chapter, fastidiously integrating the exercises into your daily life, you've reached the final pages.

This is the end—or is it the beginning?

One of my not-so-secret secret passions is music. I was raised around instruments and lyrics and late-night jam sessions, nourishing lunar food for my Pisces Moon. (Am I a Pisces Moon because I was created through song? Or is it pure coincide that the zodiac sign most directly associated with music *happens* to be my Moon? By now, you should know the answer: TANC.)

I first discovered Roxy Music when I was fourteen—their eponymous 1972 seminal album was the perfect soundtrack to my adolescence. I burned songs like "Virginia Plain" and "If There Is Something" onto blank CDs, which played on repeat as I darted around the city, smoking Camel Turkish Gold cigarettes, looking for trouble. I vaguely remember testing out a few of Roxy Music's later tracks, but back then, those songs didn't strike a chord: I needed Bryan Ferry—fresh out of art school—to affirm my purpose with perfectly pointed lyrics like "teenage rebel of the week" and a young Brian Eno, donned in peacock feathers, to defiantly twist the dials of his ancient VCS3 analog synthesizer, creating sonic badassery.

I didn't start listening to *Avalon* until I was in my late twenties, during my Saturn Return. Released in 1982 (ten years after their debut record), *Avalon* is Roxy Music's eighth and final album—though it might as well be the work of a completely different band. Gone is the youthful vibrato, the hedonistic lyrics, and the snotty experimentation (Brian Eno is also absent, having left the band in 1973). In its place, *Avalon* presents a moody soundscape that's melancholy, existential, and—frankly—fatigued.

The album opens with "More Than This," a track so complex it offers two diametrically opposed interpretations. In the chorus, Bryan Ferry sings about reaching full capacity; *there is nothing more than this*. But is the song an homage to the sublime? Has Ferry reached true contentment—is this an ode to perfection? Or is Ferry drawing a line in the sand? Perhaps "More Than This" is a boundary. The lyrics "more than this / there is nothing" serving not as a question, but rather, a statement. Is "More Than This" the beginning or the end? I believe the answer is both. The *first* song on Roxy Music's *final* album, "More Than This" is simultaneously a commencement and a conclusion.

In 2016, as I gazed upon the fragments of my life, I knew that I, too, was between worlds. I was still hurting—still trying to figure it all out. But now I knew that acknowledging my truth was embracing *everything*. The cracks, chasms, and black holes make a whole. With *Avalon* pumping through my speakers, I finally sat in discomfort and let feelings wash over me like driftwood. It wasn't submitting, I was releasing.

It's hard to believe how exponentially my life has changed over the years—it continues to transform in every possible way, a daily reminder that reality is a reflection of consciousness. I continue to work in both the astral (internal) and physical (external) realms to ensure that these dimensions are harmoniously intertwined. I treat toxic thoughts like poison ivy: I suit up in rustic hazmat and dig out the roots. Similarly, when I encounter a problem in the physical dimension—for instance, a professional disappointment or interpersonal conflict—I address it directly without letting it infiltrate my psyche. I remind myself that failures don't make *me* a failure, and the wisdom of time requires patience to uncover.

So what's more than this? Nothing.

No matter where you are in this journey, the fact that you're conscious *of* your consciousness (which is, of course, a mystical prerequisite for picking up this book in the first place—TANC!) means that you're *already* on the right path. So, at this point, I'd like to offer a few final thoughts as you continue moving forward:

1. Abracadabra

You may be familiar with the term "abracadabra"—it's often used in media depictions of stage magicians who pull bunnies out of hats or slice their lovely assistants in half. But did you know that the term is actually associated with an ancient, sacred alchemical incantation? In fact, the term is so old that its origins are unknown, though its believed that the first written documentation is over two thousand years old.[15] Whether its etymology is Hebrew, Aramaic, or Gnostic, this esoteric term loosely translates to "I create as I speak"—words become reality. As you deepen your manifestation practice, I invite you to incorporate this concept into your daily life. If you *knew* everything you said would become true, how would that shift your language? How would you shift your thoughts? Through this powerful mystical tradition, observe how you begin to replace negative, self-deprecating remarks with inspirational, higher-minded statements that materialize in the physical world. So mote it be.

2. Trust Your Magick

So, you've cultivated a specific intention, created a bridge between the astral and physical worlds, and rewired your consciousness to receive abundance . . . now what? One of the most *common* mistakes people make is micromanaging their manifestations. Perhaps you've heard the expression, "A watched pot never boils." Believe it or not, magick works the same way. Just as astrology isn't defined by a single celestial body, you're not just moving through one cycle: there are dozens upon dozens of orbits occurring simultaneously. Likewise, some manifestations may actualize faster than others. You may find that emotional shifts correspond with the Moon's twenty-eight-day orbit, while more complex intentions (such as opening a successful business) progress over longer durations of time (for example, Jupiter—the planet of expansion—has a twelve-year orbit so, when divided into quadrants, it takes about three years for a Jupiter manifestation to unfold). Of course, your birth chart (along with the current astrological transits) can help you gauge timing, but—perhaps more important—remember that manifestations fueled by anxiety, desperation, or paranoia will always yield undesirable results. I'm sorry to say, but even in the cosmos, there's no such thing as a quick fix. But hey—that's what makes it magick.

3. Appreciate Your Value Scale

If you've ever taken a drawing or black-and-white photography class, you may be familiar with the concept of a "value scale." In order for a monochromatic image to have depth, it needs to have a full tonal range, which is calibrated based on its specific "darkest dark" and "lightest light." What's important to note is that the value scale of any drawing or photograph is relative to itself. It doesn't matter whether you're rendering an eerie candlelit still-life or hyper-stylized portrait, when working within grayscale, the image will always have a self-contained "darkest dark" and "lightest light."

I reflect on this often. Although our personal "darkest darks" and "lightest lights" are calibrated to our unique experiences, we know that each individual has their own unique value scale. It's easy to impose morality on this scale, associating certain events or experiences as "good" or "bad." But if you were to look at a piece of art—say, one of Robert Mapplethorpe's exquisite flower photographs, or Caravaggio's *Bacchus*—would you condemn the shadow? No, the image is beautiful *because* of its depth, which includes its darkest dark.

Let's be honest, *none* of us have had easy journeys. Without the darkest darks, life is flat, shallow, and . . . well, boring. While there's no denying that hardships are painful—failure, tragedy, loss, and betrayal can be truly devastating, traumatic experiences—they animate us with dimensionality. And it's that complexity, that tonal depth, that makes life and art and flowers truly exquisite. So, as you continue forward, know that obstacles are just part of the bigger picture. Just as salt enhances sugar, challenges will only amplify your rewards. Nourish the shadow.

4. Invest in Others' Success

I'm so excited about your journey—I truly hope this book inspires you to tap into your fullest potential, enabling you to receive abundance beyond your wildest dreams. If all goes according to plan, I also hope that there are lots of people—just like yourself—opening portals to self-actualization. Maybe you'll even encounter some folks on social media who are celebrating their manifestation practice. Perhaps they'll be sharing transformational stories, or updates about exciting career developments, or even photos of an ultrasound—they're having a baby!

And maybe you'll want those things, too: you're also ready to break toxic cycles, step away from your energetically draining job, and meet a partner to build a family. You might feel a surge of jealousy rush through your veins, followed by a sour thought like, "She has a stupid haircut" or "Why don't good things ever happen to me?" That's fine—envy is human. But know that comparing yourself to others is a total waste of time. In fact, begrudging someone for having what you want is extremely counterproductive. By linking your desire with negativity, you're inadvertently sending confusing, mixed messages to the universe . . . and you know what that means. Yup, I'm sorry to say, but the Manifestation Café is likely to screw up your order. *Shit!*

But don't worry—there's another, *much* more productive way of addressing this emotional experience. When you encounter someone—whether virtually or in real life—who evokes jealousy, explore your reaction with compassionate curiosity. What do they have that you desire? Is it something physical? Emotional? Spiritual? Be specific. If possible, use that information to sharpen your own manifestation practice. Let envy clarify your truth. However, if you discover that these negative feelings stem from deep-seated wounds (including insecurities, inadequacies, or traumas), be sure to dig up those roots, too. Chances are, your reaction has little to do with resenting the other person and everything to do with healing yourself.

As you proceed, I invite you to practice converting your jealousy into agency by investing in others' success. When you create a link between others' achievements and your happiness, you rewire your consciousness to—quite literally—respond to abundance with *more abundance*. Practically speaking, this makes perfect sense. After all, we create our own realities, so trust that there's more than enough prosperity to go around.

As soon as you feel envy beginning to boil, visualize it forming into a clear, iridescent bubble inside your chest. In your mind's eye, imagine the bubble expanding, shifting into an oblong shape as it fills the contours of your body. Growing . . . growing . . . then—just as the bubble reaches the top of your head and the tips of your toes—let it burst into glittering golden dust, radiant warmth that infuses every corner of your being with love and gratitude and affection. All that bitterness is replaced with joy, so go ahead and like, comment, subscribe—all of the above. Now, not only are you happy for your friend, but you actually have an energetic investment in their journey. You want them to succeed, you've got skin in the game!

5. This Is Your Destiny

Like fire and gasoline, the combination of astrology and manifestation is explosive. By blending these practices, you can transform your life in extraordinarily powerful ways, generating abundance in virtually every dimension of reality. How you choose to explore this potential is up to you—the possibilities are limitless. But, as you continue moving forward, please remember that you are also part (microcosm) of a whole (macrocosm).

I hope this book will empower you to not just connect with your autonomy, but also expand your compassion, kindness, and empathy. Remember, you always get what you give: Heal yourself by helping others. Manifest abundance with reparations. Create love through having heart. You are a completely unique being—a one-of-a-kind cluster of stars and atoms and spirit. So align into your truth and bring forth that special alchemy straight from your soul. Be everything—and then be even more.

This is the beginning. This is your destiny.

✦

TABLES

✦

TABLE 1: Anatomy of a Birth Chart

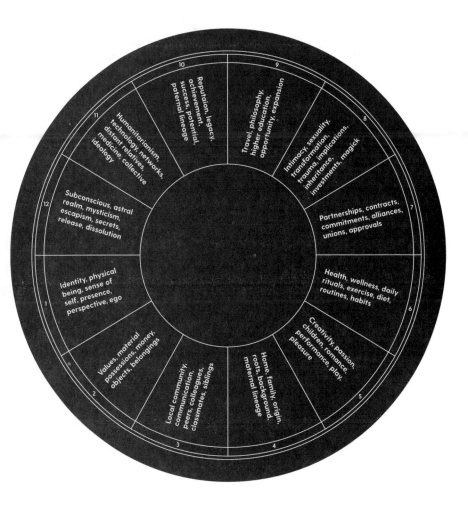

ART 1: Manifestation Flow

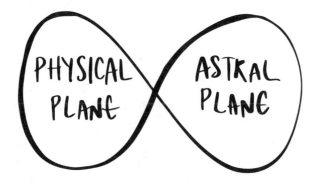

TABLE 2: Planetary Speeds

PLANET	KEYWORD	OCCUPIES ZODIAC SIGN	COMPLETE CYCLE
Moon	Emotions	2.5 days	28 days
Mercury	Communication	~1 month	~1 year
Sun	Identity	~1 month	~1 year
Venus	Values	~1 year	~1 year
Mars	Action	~6 weeks	22 months
Jupiter	Abundance	1 year	12 years
Saturn	Purpose	2.5 years	29 years
Uranus	Innovation	7 years	84 years
Neptune	Transcendence	14 years	165 years
Pluto	Rebirth	20 years	248 years

TABLE 3: Planet/Zodiac Signs/Keywords

	PROPERTIES	RISING	SUN	MOON	MERCURY	VENUS
Aries	Fire, Cardinal	Active, confident, agile	Driven, authoritative, individualistic	Zealous, restless, unbidden	Opinionated, outspoken, idealistic	Pioneering, bold, steadfast
Taurus	Earth, Fixed	Honest, present, structured	Down-to-earth, tenacious, relaxed	Cozy, stable, lush	Self-assured, stubborn, direct	Committed, luxurious, complacent
Gemini	Air, Mutable	Social, talkative, multitasker	Curious, playful, adaptable	Intellectual, cerebral, scattered	Retentive, articulate, quick	Fluid, connected, inspired
Cancer	Water, Cardinal	Protective, guarded, kind	Protective, compassionate, nurturing	Sensitive, intuitive, creative	Indirect, poetic, gentle	Nurturing, loving, classic
Leo	Fire, Fixed	Bubbly, warm, energetic	Proud, creative, generous	Loyal, intimate, adoring	Theatrical, captivating, expressive	Passionate, extreme, obsessive
Virgo	Earth, Mutable	Calm, helpful, knowledgable	Logical, practical, precise	Systematic, trustworthy, generous	Detail-oriented, organized, critical	Selective, caring, idealistic
Libra	Air, Cardinal	Elegant, magnetic, charming	Charismatic, refined, diplomatic	Relational, aesthetic, harmonious	Reflective, thoughtful, indecisive	Flirtatious, romantic, fawning
Scorpio	Water, Fixed	Intense, powerful, alluring	Ambitious, brave, honest	Deep, passionate, loyal	Investigative, pointed, illusive	Truth-seeking, committed, jealous
Sagittarius	Fire, Mutable	Witty, clever, storytelling	Inspired, expansive, philosophical	Insightful, passionate, adventurous	Blunt, optimistic, smart	Enthusiastic, playful, childlike
Capricorn	Earth, Cardinal	Stoic, entrepreneurial, mature	Hard working, diligent, grounded	Disciplined, sturdy, composed	Straightforward, logical, serious	Traditional, loyal, authentic
Aquarius	Air, Fixed	Aloof, eccentric, unique	Free-spirited, intellectual, revolutionary	Solitary, communicative, considerate	Stern, inquistive, scholarly	Nonconformist, unique, ethical
Pisces	Water, Mutable	Ethereal, enchanted, compassionate	Imaginative, creative, otherworldly	Absorbant, empathetic, artistic	Open-minded, creative, understanding	Receptive, affectionate, artistic

MARS	JUPITER	SATURN	URANUS	NEPTUNE	PLUTO
Energetic, impulsive, competitive	Adventurous, eager, egoic	Impatient, powerful, intense	Trend-setting, radical	Self-invested, instinctive	Distinctive, individualistic
Sensual, reliable, obstinate	Determined, opportunistic, qualitative	Structured, traditional, persevering	Earthy, economical	Mystical, organic	Persistent, inventive
Distractable, spirited, dynamic	Versatile, precocious, resourceful	Observant, systematic, frustrated	Social innovator, nonconformist	Novel, change-able	Versatile, destructive
Reticent, intuitive, defensive	Attentive, familial, hospitable	Responsible, devoted, wise	Expressive, clairvoyant	Whimsical, sympathetic	Conservative, guarded
Dramatic, commanding, confident	Positive, encouraging, aspirational	Proud, entitled, extreme	Original, daring, heroic	Artistic, fantastical	Demanding, egoic
Busy, perfectionism, controlling	Analytical, cautious, clever	Ernest, methodical, productive	Brilliant, sharp	Purposeful, pious	Healing, martyrdom
Indirect, careful, noncommittal	Harmonious, objective, judicious	Tactful, cooperative, fair	Cautious, collaborative	Gracious, respectful	Moderate, tempered
Strategic, powerful, penetrative	Profound, extreme, powerful	Focused, knowing, stalwart	Forceful, psychological	Mysterious, gutsy	Emotional, estoeric
Trail-blazing, fearless, spontaneous	Lucky, utopic, visionary	Independent, rebellious, boundless	Perceptive, abstract	Mythological, dogmatic	Worldly, unwieldy
Calculated, patient, resilient	Practical, strategic, successful	Motivated, goal-oriented, accomplished	Ambitious, enterprising	Discerning, faithful	Opportunistic, ruthless
Initiatory, rebellious, forward-thinking	Ingenius, socially-concious, progressive	Efficient, scientific, intelligent	Unorthodox, inventive	Reconstructive, unifying	Humanitarian, destabilizing
Structureless, adrift, infinite	Service-oriented, interconnected, spiritual	Spiritual, generative, boundless	Nuanced, transcendant	Sentient, self-sacrificing	Renewing, transformative

TABLE 4: Major Aspects

MAJOR ASPECT	SYMBOL	DEGREES	MEANING	IMPACT
Conjuction	☌	0°	Planets in the same sign	Neutral; energies blend
Opposition	☍	180°	Planets in opposite signs	Challenging; similar goals achieved different approaches
Trine	△	120°	Planets in the same element	Positive; energy is understood and validated
Square	□	90°	Planets in the same modality (excluding opposite signs)	Challenging; energy is considered from a different perspective
Sextile	✶	60°	Planets in the same polarity (excluding opposite signs)	Positive; energy is supported through mutual appreciation

TABLE 5: Rulership Chart

PLANET	MODERN RULERSHIP	TRADITIONAL RULERSHIP	TRADITIONAL DETRIMENT	TRADITIONAL EXALTATION	TRADITIONAL FALL
Sun	Leo	Leo	Aquarius	Aries	Libra
Moon	Cancer	Cancer	Capricorn	Taurus	Scorpio
Mercury	Gemini, Virgo	Gemini, Virgo	Pisces	Virgo	Pisces
Venus	Taurus, Libra	Taurus, Libra	Scorpio, Aries	Pisces	Virgo
Mars	Aries	Aries, Scorpio	Libra, Taurus	Capricorn	Cancer
Jupiter	Sagittarius	Sagittarius, Pisces	Gemini, Virgo	Cancer	Capricorn
Saturn	Capricorn	Capricorn, Aquarius	Cancer, Leo	Libra	Aries
Uranus	Aquarius	N/A	N/A	N/A	N/A
Neptune	Pisces	N/A	N/A	N/A	N/A
Pluto	Scorpio	N/A	N/A	N/A	N/A

✦

BIRTH CHARTS

✦

Birth Charts

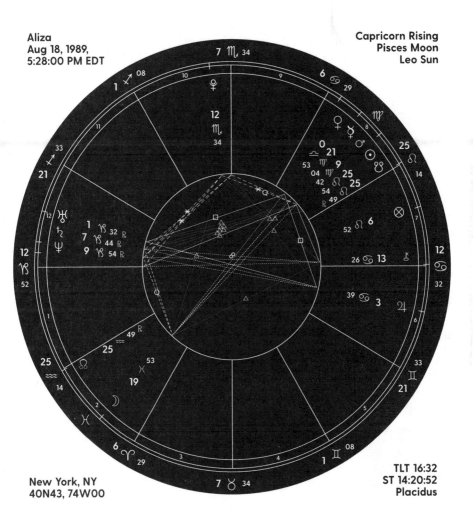

Aliza
Aug 18, 1989,
5:28:00 PM EDT

Capricorn Rising
Pisces Moon
Leo Sun

New York, NY
40N43, 74W00

TLT 16:32
ST 14:20:52
Placidus

PLATE 1

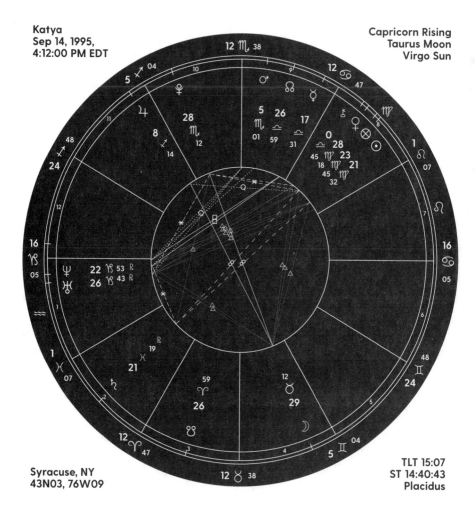

Katya
Sep 14, 1995,
4:12:00 PM EDT

Capricorn Rising
Taurus Moon
Virgo Sun

Syracuse, NY
43N03, 76W09

TLT 15:07
ST 14:40:43
Placidus

PLATE 2

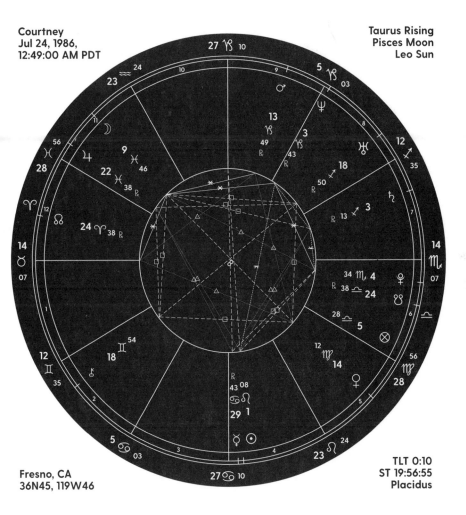

Courtney
Jul 24, 1986,
12:49:00 AM PDT

Taurus Rising
Pisces Moon
Leo Sun

Fresno, CA
36N45, 119W46

TLT 0:10
ST 19:56:55
Placidus

PLATE 3

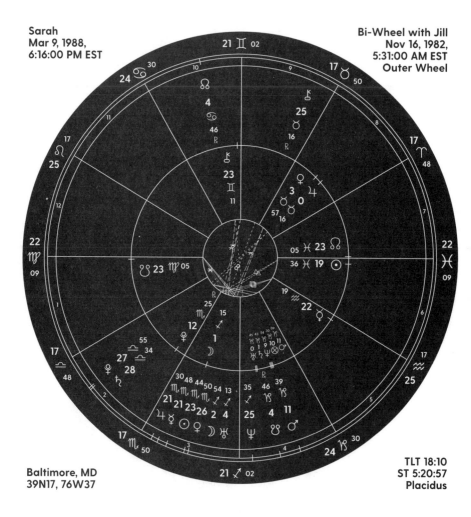

Sarah
Mar 9, 1988,
6:16:00 PM EST

Bi-Wheel with Jill
Nov 16, 1982,
5:31:00 AM EST
Outer Wheel

Baltimore, MD
39N17, 76W37

TLT 18:10
ST 5:20:57
Placidus

PLATE 4

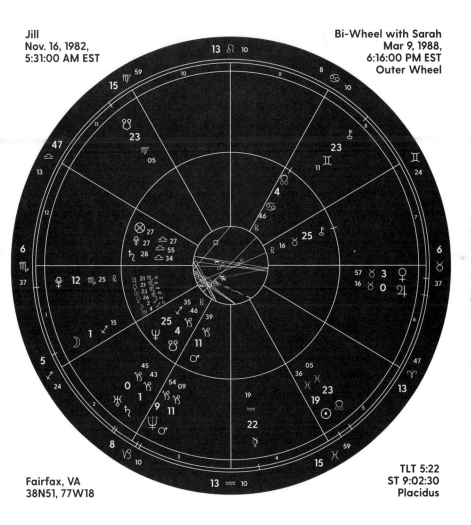

PLATE 5

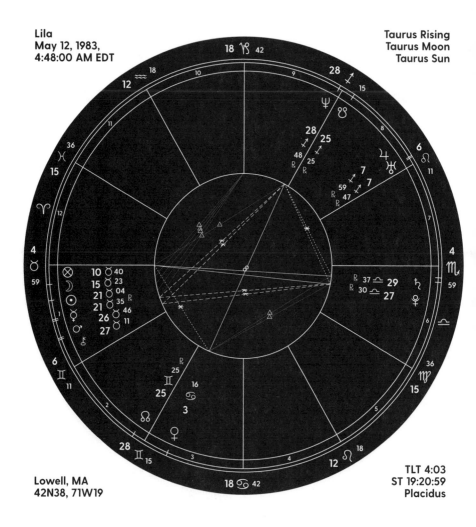

Lila
May 12, 1983,
4:48:00 AM EDT

Taurus Rising
Taurus Moon
Taurus Sun

Lowell, MA
42N38, 71W19

TLT 4:03
ST 19:20:59
Placidus

PLATE 6

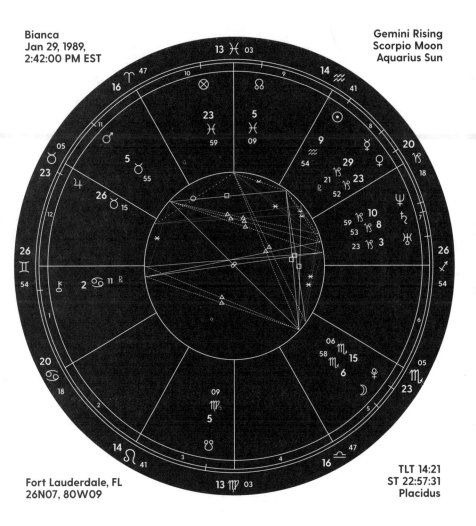

Bianca
Jan 29, 1989,
2:42:00 PM EST

**Gemini Rising
Scorpio Moon
Aquarius Sun**

Fort Lauderdale, FL
26N07, 80W09

TLT 14:21
ST 22:57:31
Placidus

PLATE 7

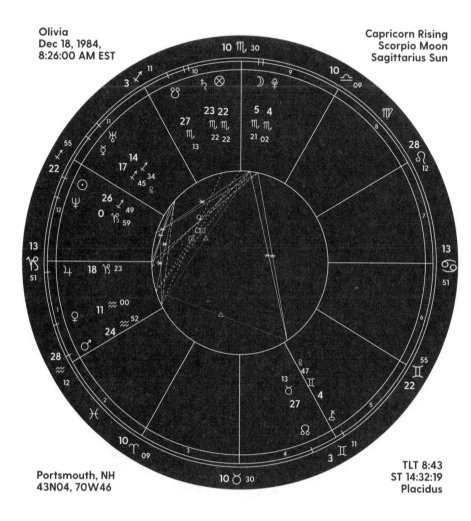

Olivia
Dec 18, 1984,
8:26:00 AM EST

Capricorn Rising
Scorpio Moon
Sagittarius Sun

Portsmouth, NH
43N04, 70W46

TLT 8:43
ST 14:32:19
Placidus

PLATE 8

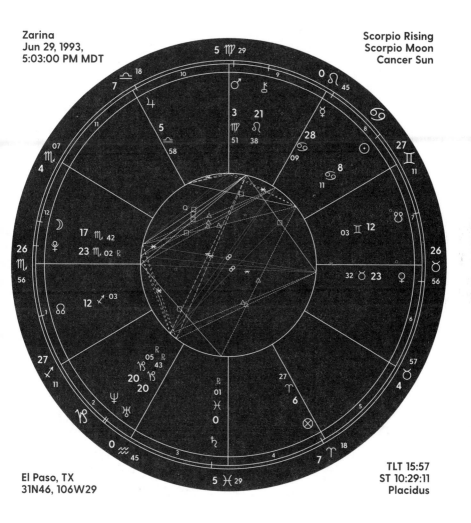

Zarina
Jun 29, 1993,
5:03:00 PM MDT

Scorpio Rising
Scorpio Moon
Cancer Sun

El Paso, TX
31N46, 106W29

TLT 15:57
ST 10:29:11
Placidus

PLATE 9

ENDNOTES

1. The ancient art of "professional mourning"—this practice is believed to originate from the choirs of Greek tragedies.
2. Tom Stoelker, "Shakespeare in Quarantine." *Fordham News.* April 21, 2020, https://news.fordham.edu/arts-and-culture/shakespeare-in-quarantine/.
3. Lynn Hayes, "William Shakespeare and the 'Grand Mutation,'" Astrodynamics!, September 6, 2007, https://www.astrodynamics.net/william-shakespeare-and-the-grand-mutation/
4. Aliza Kelly Faragher, "What This Week's Horoscope Means for You," *Allure*, August 21, 2017, https://www.allure.com/story/weekly-horoscope-week-of-august-21–2017
5. https://books.google.com/books?id=hI7h42YONQ0C&pg=RA5-PT6&lpg=RA5-PT6&dq=tycho+eclipse+1598+%22great+eclipse%22&source=bl&ots=pd-5GwsLqj&sig=ACfU3U1DgS29D0se0Wi2txhmoJqCAc0RgA&hl=en&sa=X&ved=2ahUKEwiF77n0zsPqAhX-oXIEHawBAdEQ6AEwAXoECAsQAQ#v=onepage&q=tycho%20eclipse%201598%20%22great%20eclipse%22&f=false
6. In western (tropical) astrology, the zodiac signs share names with constellations—but the signs themselves are *not* constellations, they are sections of the sky. Every few months, the Internet gets flooded with stories claiming NASA announced the Earth has shifted, a new constellation (Ophiuchus) has been revealed, and (gasp!) there are actually thirteen zodiac signs. But the Earth is *always* shifting (tropical astrology is a fixed system, meaning it doesn't adjust per the Earth's axial precession), Ophiuchus has *always* existed (there are, in fact, eighty-eight classical constellations) and, accordingly, there only will ever be twelve zodiac signs with the tropical tradition.
7. Sun sign astrology—also known as "star sign" or "horoscope astrology" is based on the position of the Sun at an individual's moment of birth.
8. Horary astrology is a particular branch of astrology that's designed to answer "yes or no" questions—it's sort of like a Magic 8-Ball, except it's an extremely specialized practice that's notoriously difficult to learn.

9. Oh, this is your friendly reminder that I'm *not* a medical professional: psychological needs should be treated by a professional—my vantage is astrological.

10. The Sun and Moon are referred to as "Luminaries."

11. Also referred to as the Midheaven or the MC, this is the highest point in the sky, which usually occurs around noon.

12. "Aspects" refer to the connections made by two or more celestial bodies.

13. The Rising Sign (or "Ascendant") is the zodiac sign emerging on the eastern horizon at your moment of birth.

14. Both psychology and astrology address the human condition, which is why astrologers use language that is often rooted in psychology. Please note, however, that I'm using these words to describe character archetypes—not to psychoanalyze.

15. It was first recorded by Quintus Serenus Sammonicus (physician to Roman Emperor Caracalla) in the medical book *Liber Medicinalis* (also known as *De Medicina Praecepta Saluberrima*). Alchemists would etch this word into talismans, using the letters to create an upside-down triangle (in many magic traditions, pyramids or cones are used to direct energy) that would be worn like a necklace for both healing and protection.

ACKNOWLEDGMENTS

To Helen Grossman, my co-founder, co-pilot, co-Leo. Thank you, from the bottom of my heart, for your tenacity, brilliance, and laughter. Thank you for believing in our magic, giving me the confidence to find my voice, and for helping me navigate Los Angeles (through George's Eyes). I love you so very much. Annabel Gat, thank you for your incredible wisdom, generosity, and hospitality. You taught me how to become an astrologer, but perhaps even more important, you showed me that there's always more room at the table. I am forever grateful. Adam Krasner, thank you for taking a chance on a baby astrologer, and for all of these wonderful years of teamwork, friendship, and reverse psychology techniques to help me find my way. Paula Lee Young, for swooping in at the eleventh hour like a true Virgo goddess. To my sisters at *Cosmopolitan* magazine, especially Mia Lardiere, Jessica Pels, Erika Smith, and Jen Ortiz. My closest confidants: Emily Meade, Sahara Ghafari, Blaine Morris, Rachel Schwartz, Lara Ewald, Lulu Obermayer, Eli Gold, Lallie Jones, Rachel Troy, Henry Moskowitz, Sofia Szamosi, Johnny Siera Orlee-Rose Strauss, Hannah Becker. My therapists through the years: Cindy Glickstein, Sharyn Wolf, Nathan Rice, Caitlin Tonda. My teachers, mentors, and colleagues: Anne Ortelee, Tali and Ophi Edut, Steph Koyfman, Jake Register, Liana Mack, Maia Orion, Kesaine Walker, Jessica Lanyandoo, Alby Toribio, Caitlin Adams, Serita Fontanesi. My team: Isabel Gallant, Brandi Bowles, Ana Mijich, Tori Botsford, Katrin Ree. My crew at St. Martin's Press, especially my editor, Eileen Rothschild, who brought this work to life. My Golden family, especially my magical Mommy and Grandma Anita. The Golden-West family—especially Jeremy and Glory, the original astrologers. My Faragher family, especially my dad, Rosie, and Daisy. The Constellation Club and all of my clients, each of whom deserves the Moon and stars. And finally, Luke Schwartz, my soul mate and life partner. Before you, it was all theoretical. Your love gives me the strength to trust the magic of the stars—all these years later—I still cannot believe you're real. Love you forever.